Composition through grammar 2

Muriel Higgins

Longman

Introduction

This is the second book in a composition course which takes students to intermediate level. It offers the student written practice of common grammatical structures and shows how these can be used in connected writing from sentence to paragraph level.

There are fourteen four-page units in the book, each focusing on a grammatical topic. Each unit is divided into four parts:

- **Part A** first presents a text, often in dialogue form. Students' attention is directed to an area of grammar by exercises which ask for information to be retrieved from the text. This allows students to concentrate on meaning and write correct sentences without having to manipulate the structure.

- **Part B** practises one aspect of the central grammar topic.

- **Part C** practises a further aspect of the topic.

- **Part D** begins by drawing attention to areas which are important for correct writing: spelling, punctuation and word study. The final writing practice section moves from the controlled use of material presented earlier in the unit towards free use in more open-ended writing in which students are encouraged to write about themselves and their own circumstances.

Information for study and reference is presented in boxes headed 'Notice'. These focus attention on the main points being practised and explain them clearly and concisely.

An answer key for the controlled exercises is provided at the back of the book.

Contents

UNIT 1 Comparison of adjectives

Part A Read and answer

1 Read this passage:

Who stole the baby?

This afternoon a woman stole a baby outside a supermarket. Joan was coming out of the supermarket, and she saw the woman. A policeman is asking Joan about the woman now.

POLICEMAN: Look at this picture, please. Is that the same woman?

JOAN: Well, I don't think so. No, that isn't the woman I saw. She had shorter hair. Her hair was curlier than that, too.

POLICEMAN: Did you see her face?

JOAN: Oh yes. Her face was rounder than that.

POLICEMAN: Anything else?

JOAN: Wait a minute. Her nose was different. It wasn't so short. Yes, she had a longer nose than that. It was thinner, too.

POLICEMAN: Good.

JOAN: Her mouth wasn't like that, either. It was much bigger. Her mouth was much wider.

POLICEMAN: All right. Now can you remember anything else about the woman you saw?

JOAN: She looked cleverer. I think she looked more intelligent than this woman.

2 Find the sentences with these adjectives:

EXAMPLE
bigger
It was much bigger.

1 cleverer   2 curlier   3 longer
4 more intelligent   5 rounder   6 shorter
7 thinner   8 wider

3 Complete the policeman's notes.

The policeman made some notes while he was talking to Joan. Find the words he wrote.

1 Hair : shorter, curlier
2 Face :
3 Nose :
4 Mouth :
5 Appearance :

4 Who stole the baby?

The policeman showed this picture to Joan. She said it wasn't the same woman. She told him how the woman she saw was different. Which woman did Joan see – A, B, C or D?

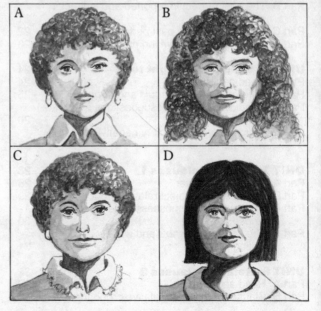

4

Part B Comparison with **er/est**; comparison of **good** and **bad**

1 Notice how to spell regular comparatives and superlatives with **er** and **est**.

> The general rule is add **er/est**:
> *short, shorter, shortest; long, longer, longest*
> Words ending in **e** add **r/st**:
> *wide, wider, widest; brave, braver, bravest*
> Words ending in **y** have **ier/iest**:
> *busy, busier, busiest; tidy, tidier, tidiest*
> Words with short vowels double the last letter:
> *hot, hotter, hottest; thin, thinner, thinnest*

2 Write sentences with comparatives.

EXAMPLE
English/maths/easy
English is easier than maths.
OR *Maths is easier than English.*
(You decide.)

1 icecream/chocolate cake/nice
2 dogs/cats/friendly
3 January/July/hot
4 languages/science subjects/easy
5 apples/potatoes/cheap
6 cars/bicycles/safe

3 Answer in sentences with superlatives.

EXAMPLE
Who is the tallest person in your family?
My father/mother/sister/brother is the tallest person in my family.

1 Who is the tallest person in your family?
2 What is the biggest city in your country?
3 Who is the quietest person in your class?
4 And who is the noisiest?
5 What is the longest river in your country?
6 Who has the loudest voice in your family?

4 Complete with the right form of the adjective.

EXAMPLE
London is a __ city. It's one of the __ cities in the world. (large)
London is a large city. It's one of the largest cities in the world.

1 The Sahara Desert is very __. It's one of the __ places in the world. (hot)
2 Canada is a __ country. But Russia is __ than Canada. (big)
3 The __ country in South America is Brazil. It's much __ than all the other countries. (large)
4 London and Paris are both __ cities. Some people think that Paris is __ than London. (busy)

5 Notice:

good	better	best
bad	worse	worst

6 Look at the marks and complete the sentences.

NAME	MARKS		
Anne	85		
Bob	43		
Charles	71		
Doris	54		
Eva	36		

EXAMPLE
Anne got the __ mark.
Anne got the best mark.

1 Her mark was __ than all the other marks.
2 Eva got a __ mark. Her mark was the __.
3 Bob's mark was __ than Eva's, but it wasn't very
4 Bob was __ than Anne, Charles and Doris.
5 Anne's mark was the __, and Eva's was the __.

Part C Comparison with **more** and **most**

1 Notice:

> Longer adjectives form the comparative with
> **more**, and the superlative with **most**:
>
> difficult   more difficult   most difficult
> interesting   more interesting   most interesting
> (See Exercise 1 Part D for help in choosing
> **er/est** or **more/most**.)

2 Give your opinion.

EXAMPLE
__ is more interesting than __. (geography, history)
Geography is more interesting than history.
OR *History is more interesting than geography.*
(You decide.)

1 __ is more useful than __. (geography, history)
2 __ are more intelligent than __. (girls, boys)
3 __ is more famous than __. (Elvis Presley,
   John Lennon)
4 __ are more beautiful than __. (flowers, trees)
5 __ is more difficult than __. (being clever, being
   nice)
6 __ are more important than __. (managers,
   workers)

3 Answer in sentences.

EXAMPLE
Which is more dangerous: skiing or swimming?
Skiing is more dangerous than swimming.

1 Which is more interesting: colour TV or black
   and white TV?
2 Which is more difficult: learning a foreign
   language or learning your own language?
3 Which is more popular: tennis or football?
4 Which are more expensive: tomatoes or potatoes?
5 Which is more helpful: a big dictionary or a
   small dictionary?
6 Which are more intelligent: animals or people?

4 Give true answers with superlatives.

EXAMPLE
What's the most popular sport in your country?
*(Football/Running) is the most popular sport in my
country.*

1 What's the most popular sport in your country?
2 What's the most interesting city?
3 What's the most exciting film you have ever
   seen?
4 Who is the most intelligent person in your
   family?
5 What's the most interesting school subject?
6 What's the most difficult subject?

5 Complete with the right form of the adjective.

EXAMPLE
Football is a __ game. Perhaps it's __ game in the
world. (popular)
*Football is a popular game. Perhaps it's the most
popular game in the world.*

1 Arabic and Chinese are __ languages to learn.
   Chinese is probably __ than Arabic. (difficult)
2 Paris is one of the __ cities in Europe. Some
   people say Paris is the __ city in the world.
   (exciting)
3 Fruit is usually __ than vegetables. In most
   countries meat is __ food, but in some places fish
   is __ than meat. (expensive)

6 Write true sentences about the different
   subjects that you study.

1 I think that (subject) is more interesting than
   (subject).
2 (name) doesn't agree. He/She says that (subject)
   is the most interesting (subject).
3 In my opinion, (subject) is the most difficult, but
   (name) thinks that (subject) is more difficult.

Part D The choice of comparative and superlative forms; writing practice

1 Notice these comparative and superlative forms:

> Use **er/est**:
> 1 with adjectives of one syllable: *hot*.
> 2 with adjectives of two syllables ending in **-le, -ow, -y** (**y** changes to **i**) or **er**: *gentle, narrow, happy, clever*.
>
> Use **more/most**:
> 1 with adjectives of three or more syllables: *difficult, intelligent*.
> 2 with adjectives ending in **-ing, -ed, -ful, -less** or **-ous**: *boring, surprised, useful, careless, famous*.
>
> Note that some adjectives can have **er/est** or **more/most**:
> polite: *politer* or *more polite, politest* or *most polite*
> handsome: *handsomer, handsomest,* or *more/most handsome*

2 Write the comparative and superlative forms of these adjectives:

1 angry   2 annoyed   3 early   4 healthy
5 helpful   6 exciting   7 marvellous 8 shallow
9 simple   10 strange   11 tiring   12 useless

3 Write a paragraph about Pat and Matt by choosing the sentences which are true.

Pat   1m 75cms   69 kgs   Matt   1m 75cms   69 kgs

Patrick and Matthew Smart are twins. Their friends call them Pat and Matt.

1 a Pat and Matt are the same height.
  b Matt is taller than Pat.
2 a One of them is heavier than the other.
  b They are the same weight, too.
3 a There isn't any difference in their appearance.
  b There isn't much difference in their appearance.
4 a The only thing that's different is their hair.
  b Pat's hair is exactly the same as Matt's.
5 a Pat's hair is longer than Matt's.
  b Pat's hair is shorter than Matt's.

4 Write a similar paragraph about two people you know.

Sentence 1 says who they are: are they friends/sisters/brothers etc?
Sentence 2 is about their height.
Sentence 3 is about their weight.
Sentence 4 is about their appearance: is there a lot of difference, or not much difference?
Sentence 5 begins: *One thing that is different is . . .*
Sentence 6 says more about the thing that is different.

5 Write another paragraph by completing these sentences about their interests.

1 (name) is more interested in ___ than (name), and he/she is better at ___ than (name).
2 But he/she isn't as good at ___ as (name) is.
3 (name) thinks that ___ is the most exciting sport/game/pastime, but (name) doesn't agree. He/She says that ___ is much more enjoyable.

UNIT 2 Too and enough; so . . . that

Part A Read and answer

1 Read this passage:

Football special

INTERVIEWER: Now here's the result of this afternoon's important match: Liverham nil, Tottenpool two. The managers of both teams are here with me. Here's Dick Mills, the Tottenpool manager. How do you feel, Dick?

DICK MILLS: Great. Our team played well enough to win the World Cup! They were so fast that Liverham never got the ball. All right, Liverham almost scored at the beginning. But our players were so good that Liverham never got another chance.

INTERVIEWER: Well, congratulations, Dick. But now let's talk to Peter Evans, the Liverham manager.

PETER EVANS: Dick's right about one thing. Liverham didn't play well enough to win. They played too slowly. They didn't work hard enough. But it isn't true that we never got the ball, Dick. We weren't fast enough to score a goal, that's all. It really was a disappointing match for us.

INTERVIEWER: Thank you, Peter, and better luck next time. We all hope that Liverham will play well enough to win their big match in Spain next week. Good luck!

2 Complete the sentences with **Tottenpool** or **Liverham**.

EXAMPLE
__ were so fast that __ never got the ball.
Tottenpool were so fast that Liverham never got the ball.

1 __ didn't play well enough to win.
2 __ almost scored at the beginning.
3 The __ players were so good that __ never got another chance.
4 __ didn't work hard enough.
5 __ played well enough to win the World Cup!
6 __ weren't fast enough to score.
7 Everyone hopes __ will play well enough to win in Spain.

3 Find the sentences with these phrases:

EXAMPLE
played well enough
Our team played well enough to win the World Cup.

1 so good that   2 fast enough
3 too slowly   4 hard enough
5 so fast that   6 will play well enough
7 not (n't) . . . well
  enough

4 Find the sentences that give these ideas:

EXAMPLE
Liverham didn't play well. They didn't win.
Liverham didn't play well enough to win.

1 Our team played well. Perhaps they can win the World Cup.
2 Tottenpool were very quick. The other team never got the ball.
3 Liverham weren't very quick. They didn't score a goal.
4 Tottenpool were very good. Liverham never had another chance.
5 We hope Liverham will play well next week. We hope they will win.

Part B Too and enough with adjectives and adverbs

1 Notice the word order:

> **too** + adjective/adverb,
> (**not**) + adjective/adverb + **enough**
> *The Liverham players were too slow.*
> *They played too slowly.*
> *They weren't good enough.*
> *They didn't play well enough.*

2 Choose the phrases with the same meaning.

EXAMPLE
too cold = not warm enough

too	cold low narrow old shallow short slow young	not	deep high long new old quick warm wide	enough

3 Give the right reasons, using the phrases in Exercise 2.

EXAMPLE
Don't go swimming today. The water . . .
The water is too cold. It isn't warm enough.

1 You mustn't dive into the river. The water . . .
2 Tommy wants to go to school, but he is only three, and he can't. He . . .
3 Liverham lost the match. They . . .

4 Peter's car is ten years old, so don't buy it. It . . .
5 I like these trousers, but I'm not going to buy them. They . . .
6 Don't put your car in my garage. The garage . . .
7 That chair . . . . You won't be able to reach the ceiling.

4 Notice:

too+adjective/adverb (**not**)+adjective/adverb+**enough**	**to**+infinitive

5 Put two ideas into one sentence.

EXAMPLE
Liverham didn't play well. They didn't win.
Liverham didn't play well enough to win.
They were slow. They didn't get the ball.
They were too slow to get the ball.

1 Tottenpool played well. Maybe they'll win the cup.
2 The other team didn't work hard. They didn't get a goal.
3 They were tired. That's why they didn't work hard.
4 They had been busy. They couldn't practise.
5 We hope they'll play well. We hope they'll win next week.

6 Think of an answer with **too** or **not . . . enough**.

EXAMPLE
Why aren't you the Prime Minister?
I'm not clever enough to be the Prime Minister.
OR *I'm too young to be the Prime Minister.*
(You decide.)

1 Why aren't you the Prime Minister?
2 You should be an Olympic athlete!
3 Why don't you write a book?
4 Maybe you should read the news on television.
5 Why aren't you a famous singer or songwriter?

Part C So . . . that with adjectives and adverbs

1 Notice the pattern:

> **so** + adjective/adverb + **that**:
> *She's so busy that she can't take a holiday.*
> *Liverham played so badly that their manager was angry.*
> Note also these examples with **much, many** and **few**.
> *He has so much money that he can't spend it all.*
> *There were so many people in the bus that we had to stand.*
> *There are so few tourists that there aren't many hotels.*

2 Write one sentence with **so . . . that**.

EXAMPLE
I'm busy. I can't come with you.
I'm so busy that I can't come with you.

1 It's wet. You'll need an umbrella.
2 That dress is expensive. Joan can't afford it.
3 The film was boring. We came home.
4 I worked hard. I got very hungry.
5 The boy answered quietly. The teacher couldn't hear him.
6 Mrs Brown's suitcase was heavy. She couldn't carry it.
7 It was late when they arrived. They had to take a taxi.

3 Choose the right word to complete the sentence.

EXAMPLE
The children were so __ that their teacher got angry. (noisy, noisily)
The children were so noisy that their teacher got angry.

1 They were playing so __ that they didn't hear him. (noisy, noisily)
2 The teacher got so __ that he began to shout. (angry, angrily)
3 He shouted so __ that the children finally heard him. (loud, loudly)
4 They became so __ that he stopped shouting. (quiet, quietly)
5 The children listened so __ that he was sorry he'd shouted. (quiet, quietly)

4 Decide what happened and write one sentence.

EXAMPLE
Last night you were reading a very exciting book. What happened?
My book was so exciting that I couldn't sleep. OR *My book was so exciting that I read it until midnight.* (You decide.)

1 You saw a frightening film last week. (Begin: *The film . . .*)
2 When you came home yesterday, you were very hungry.
3 You were very tired this morning.
4 One of your friends felt ill yesterday. (Begin with his/her name.)
5 When you went on holiday, your suitcase was heavy.

5 Choose the sentences that are true for you.

1 a Films in English are so difficult that I can't understand them.
  b I'm good enough at English to understand English films.
2 a I know so many English-speakers that I often speak English.
  b It's so difficult to meet English-speakers that I hardly ever speak English.
3 a There are so many English and American tourists in our country that it's important to speak English.
  b There are so few English-speaking visitors that we don't need to learn English.
4 a English is so important that many people learn it.
  b In our country, other languages are more important than English.

Part D Adjectives and adverbs with the same form; writing practice

1 Notice these adjectives and adverbs:

> We can form adverbs by adding **-ly** to adjectives: slow, *slowly*; quiet, *quietly*, etc. (But remember that some adjectives end with **-ly** : *lovely, friendly*. Not all words that end in **-ly** are adverbs.)
>
> There are also some adverbs that have the same form as adjectives:
>
> | | | |
> |---|---|---|
> | hard | *He is a hard worker.* | *He works hard.* |
> | fast | *This is a fast car.* | *Anne always drives fast.* |
> | late | *We were late.* | *We arrived late.* |
> | early | *The early train leaves at six.* | *It leaves very early.* |
> | first | *Jim won the first prize.* | *Who came first in the race?* |
> | last | *This isn't the last sentence.* | *Peter came last in the race.* |

2 Choose the right words to complete the sentences.

EXAMPLE
Mr Black is a fast driver, and he sometimes drives too fast.
But his wife always drives very ___ because she has a ___ car. (slow, slowly)
But his wife always drives very slowly because she has a slow car.

1 When they go somewhere, he usually arrives early. Mrs Black drives so ___ that she often arrives ___. (late, slow, slowly)
2 He thinks she is too ___ , and she thinks he isn't ___ enough! (fast, slow, slowly)
3 She says he drives so fast that he's ___ , but he says he always drives ___. (dangerous, dangerously, safe, safely)
4 He often tells her that fast drivers are ___ drivers, and that ___ drivers often drive very ___. (badly, good, slow, slowly, well)

3 Prepare for writing.

Last month, some of your friends had a really terrible holiday. What happened, and why was it so terrible that they came home early?

EXAMPLE
They couldn't sleep. Why not?
The rooms were too hot.
OR *The beds weren't soft enough.*
OR *The hotel was so noisy that no one could sleep.*
(You decide the reason.)

1 They didn't enjoy the food.
2 They never went swimming.
3 They didn't buy anything.
4 They didn't like the town.
5 They didn't like the manager of the hotel.
6 The weather was bad.

4 Complete part of the letter your friends wrote to the travel agency.

> Last month we went to the ...
> Hotel in ... for ... weeks.
> Everything was so bad that we
> left after ... days. The food
> in the hotel restaurant was
> awful: the waiters were
> too ... and we always had to
> wait for our meals. When the
> food came, it wasn't ... enough,
> either. We couldn't sleep at
> night, because the rooms
> weren't ... enough, and the
> beds were much too ... . We
> spoke to the manager about this,
> and he was so ... that we
> decided to leave.

5 Write a similar paragraph, using your ideas from Exercise 3.

UNIT 3 The passive

Part A Read and answer

1 Read this passage:

Here is the news

Good evening. Tonight the main news is about the weather. Storms are reported in all parts of the country.

In Scotland and the north, many roads are closed because of high winds. Two main roads near Glasgow are blocked by trees.

In the south, too, heavy rain and storms are reported. Near Dover, fifty houses have been flooded, and last night a lorry on a motorway was blown over by the wind.

In the east, high tides have flooded many areas. Many small boats have been lost, and this morning one boat was found two miles inland. High tides are expected again tonight.

Things are better in the west. But two villages have been flooded by a river. Four people were rescued by helicopter this afternoon.

And the forecast? More storms are expected tomorrow.

2 Find the sentences with these meanings:

EXAMPLE
There is news about bad weather everywhere.
Storms are reported in all parts of the country.

1 Trees block two main roads in Scotland.
2 People expect more high tides tonight.
3 A helicopter helped to save four people.
4 There will probably be more storms tomorrow.

3 Find the missing words.

EXAMPLE
Many roads __ __ because of __ __.
Many roads are closed because of high winds.

1 Heavy rain and storms __ __ in __ __.
2 Fifty houses __ __ __ near __.
3 A lorry on a motorway __ __ __ by __ __.
4 Many small boats __ __ __.
5 One boat __ __ two __ inland.

4 Choose the right words from the boxes to complete this summary of the news (one sentence for each paragraph).

EXAMPLE
Storms *are reported everywhere*.

1 Storms . . .   2 Many roads . . .

3 In the south, . . .   4 High tides . . .

5 Two villages . . .   6 More storms . . .

are reported	everywhere.
have flooded	tomorrow.
are closed	in the west.
are expected	is reported.
heavy rain	parts of the east coast.
have been flooded	in Scotland.

Part B The passive in the simple present and simple past tenses

1 Notice:

> The passive is formed with parts of the verb **to be** and a past participle:
>
> Simple present: *Bad weather is expected tomorrow.*
> *Helicopters are used by the police.*
>
> Simple past: *An accident was caused by the wind.*
> *Two main roads were blocked by trees.*

2 Rewrite these sentences in the passive. Do not include a phrase with **by**.

EXAMPLE
Someone took the lorry-driver to hospital.
The lorry-driver was taken to hospital.

1 Someone examined him.
2 Someone told his wife about the accident.
3 Someone brought her to the hospital.
4 The doctors allowed the lorry-driver to go home.
5 They advised him to go to bed and rest.
6 Someone ordered a taxi.
7 The taxi took the man and his wife home.

3 Rewrite in the passive, using a phrase with **by** at the end of the sentence.

EXAMPLE
A young woman saw the accident.
The accident was seen by a young woman.

1 High winds caused the accident.
2 Trees blocked two main roads.
3 The police closed many roads.
4 Sea water flooded many areas.
5 Two children found a small boat in a field.
6 A river flooded two villages.
7 The police used a helicopter.

4 Answer with two sentences.

EXAMPLE
Is meat sold by a baker or a butcher?
Meat isn't sold by a baker. It's sold by a butcher.

1 In a restaurant, are meals prepared by a waiter or a cook?
2 At home, is most of the cooking done by you or by someone else?
3 Are you taught English by a man or by a woman?
4 Is your homework usually corrected by your teacher or by other students?
5 In your country, are buses usually driven by men or by women?
6 What about aeroplanes? Are they usually flown by men or by women?

5 Active or passive? Choose the right form of the simple past.

EXAMPLE
Many places in Britain __ yesterday. (flood)
Many places in Britain were flooded yesterday.

1 High tides on the east coast __ many areas. (flood)
2 Many fields __ by sea water. (cover)
3 One farmer __ by a reporter. (interview)
4 This is what he __ the reporter. (tell)
5 'Last night I __ twelve dead cows. (find)
6 This morning many more dead animals __. (find)
7 The water __ all my land.' (flood)
8 The reporter also __ some other farmers in the same area. (interview)

Part C The passive with other tenses

1 Notice these passive forms:

> Present perfect: **has/have** + **been** + past participle:
> *Heavy rain has been reported in the south.*
> *Many fields have been flooded by sea water.*
>
> Future: **will/won't** + **be** + past participle:
> *Some roads will be closed for two days.*
> *They won't be opened until Friday.*

2 Rewrite these sentences in the passive:

EXAMPLE
In Scotland, trees have blocked many roads. (+ by)
In Scotland, many roads have been blocked by trees.

1 The police have closed these roads. (+ by)
2 They won't open the roads until they have moved the trees. (Rewrite both clauses.)
3 People have lost many small boats in the east.
4 Sea water has flooded many farms. (+ by)
5 The police have used helicopters in Wales.
6 They have asked the army to help.
7 The army will send some soldiers to Wales tonight.

3 Complete this story by choosing the right words:

EXAMPLE
A very old ship has __ by the storms.
(moved, been moved)
A very old ship has been moved by the storms.

1 Part of a ship has __ in the sea near Dover. (see, been seen)
2 Historians have __ that it may be the *Isabella*. (said, been said)
3 The *Isabella* is a Spanish ship which __ about 1585. (lost, was lost)
4 When the sea is calmer, divers will __ down to explore the ship. (send, be sent)
5 The divers will __ some photographs. (take, be taken)
6 These photographs will __ with special cameras. (take, be taken)
7 A museum in London has __ a picture of the *Isabella*. (found, been found)
8 The photographs will __ with the picture. (compare, be compared)
9 If it is the *Isabella*, perhaps some gold will __. (find, be found)
10 Many people have __ gold in other Spanish ships. (found, been found)

4 Answer in sentences.

EXAMPLE
Where has this ship been seen?
It has been seen in the sea near Dover.

1 When was the *Isabella* lost?
2 Who will the ship be explored by?
3 What will be needed to take photographs?
4 What has been found in a museum?
5 Perhaps something will be found on the *Isabella* – what?
6 Where has gold already been found?

5 Choose the true sentences.

EXAMPLE
The ship has already been explored (*not true*)
The ship hasn't been explored yet. (*true*)

1 a Historians have been asked about the ship.
  b No opinions have been given by historians.
2 a Divers have already been sent down.
  b Divers haven't been sent down yet.
3 a Special underwater cameras will be needed.
  b No special cameras will be needed.
4 a A picture of the *Isabella* has been found.
  b No pictures of the *Isabella* have ever been found.
5 a Gold was sometimes carried on Spanish ships.
  b Gold was never carried on Spanish ships.

Part D The use of passives in headlines; writing practice

1 Notice this use of the passive:

Newspaper headlines often use a short form of the passive. For example, an article about some diamonds which have been stolen has the headline DIAMONDS STOLEN. If the thief is caught, the headline is THIEF CAUGHT. This means that the thief has been caught; it doesn't mean that the thief caught someone.

2 Choose the right headline.

EXAMPLE

On Saturday the Queen opened a new theatre in . . .

QUEEN OPENED or THEATRE OPENED?
Theatre opened

1 The girl who disappeared from her home on Friday has been found near . . .

CHILD FOUND or CHILD LOST?

2 A new television factory with 120 jobs will open next month, the manager said yesterday in . . .

JOBS PLANNED or MANAGER PLANNED?

3 Thieves took gold and diamonds worth a million pounds from a hotel in . . .

THIEVES TAKEN or JEWELS STOLEN?

3 Read Part A Exercise 1 again and answer these questions:

1 How many paragraphs are there?
2 Which paragraph tells you something general?
3 How many paragraphs are about particular places?
4 What is the last paragraph about?

4 Prepare for writing by thinking about your country. Make short notes.

1 What kind of weather is important enough to be in the news:
   – very cold weather with a lot of snow?
   – a heatwave (unusually hot weather with very high temperatures)?
   – too much rain, or not enough rain?
   – storms and very high winds?
2 What are the results of bad weather? Are roads closed? Is land flooded? Are houses damaged? Are animals or crops (things that farmers grow) lost?
3 Four areas of Britain are described: the north, the south, the east and the west. Can your country be described like this? Decide how to describe it.

5 Write a news story about bad weather in your country.

The first paragraph is the introduction. Look at Part A Exercise 1 again, and change words to describe your situation.
The middle paragraphs are about different parts of the country. You don't have to write about four parts. It depends on your country. Write two to four sentences in each paragraph.
The last paragraph is the weather forecast.

UNIT 4 Reported and indirect statements

Part A Read and answer

1 Read this passage:

Mary Patel takes her mother to the doctor

DR: Good morning. Are you Mrs Patel?
MARY: No, this is Mrs Patel. I'm her daughter. I've come to help her. You see, my mother understands English all right. But she doesn't speak it very well. I'll tell you what she says.
DR: Right. Now, what's her problem?
MARY: She gets very bad headaches.
DR: How often?
MARY: She says she gets them almost every day.
DR: Where does it hurt, exactly?
MARY: Above her eyes.
DR: Does your mother sleep well?
MARY: No. She says she never sleeps well. She doesn't go to sleep easily, and she often wakes up during the night.
DR: I see. Now listen. I'll give your mother something for her headaches, and some sleeping pills. But I want to see her again. You must bring her back next week.
MARY: All right. Thank you very much, doctor.

2 Find the exact words they use.

EXAMPLE
Mary says she is Mrs Patel's daughter.
I'm her daughter.

1 Mary tells the doctor that she has come to help her mother.
2 She explains that her mother doesn't speak English very well.
3 She says she'll tell the doctor what her mother says.
4 The doctor says he'll give Mrs Patel two kinds of medicine.
5 He says he wants to see Mrs Patel again.
6 He tells Mary she must bring Mrs Patel back next week.

3 How does Mary report her mother's statements?

EXAMPLE
MRS PATEL: I get very bad headaches.
MARY: *She gets very bad headaches.*

1 I get them almost every day.
2 I never sleep well.
3 I don't go to sleep easily.
4 I often wake up during the night.

4 Complete each sentence with one or more words from Exercise 1.

EXAMPLE
Mary told the doctor that she was Mrs Patel's . . . .
Mary told the doctor that she was Mrs Patel's daughter.

1 She said her mother understood . . . , but she didn't speak . . . .
2 Mary said her mother got very . . . .
3 Mrs Patel said that she never slept . . . .
4 She said she often woke up . . . .
5 The doctor said he'd give Mrs Patel something . . . and some . . . .
6 He said he wanted to . . . .
7 He told Mary that she must bring her mother back . . . .

Part B Reported and indirect statements with present tense introductory verbs

1 Notice:

> Sentences usually change when they are reported:
>
> 'I feel ill.'   *Mrs Patel says she feels ill.*
> 'I've come to   *Mary tells the doctor that*
> help my   *she's come to help her*
> mother.'   *mother.*
> 'I'll give you   *The doctor says he'll give her*
> some pills.'   *some pills.*
>
> Pronouns, the person of the verb and possessive adjectives must be changed to keep the correct meaning (*Mrs Patel says I feel ill.* means something different).
> After a present tense introductory verb (**says, tells,** etc), the tense of the verb is not changed. In speech and informal writing, **that** is often omitted.

2 Report these statements. Do not use **that**.

EXAMPLE
My headaches have stopped. (Mrs Patel says)
Mrs Patel says her headaches have stopped.

1 I feel much better. (She tells the doctor)
2 I want to examine your eyes. (The doctor says)
3 You must go to the eye hospital. (He tells Mrs Patel)
4 I don't want to go to the hospital. (Mrs Patel says)
5 I'll phone the hospital now. (The doctor says)

3 Report these statements with **tells . . . that**:

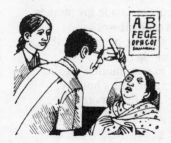

EXAMPLE
EYE DOCTOR: You must have an operation, Mrs Patel.
The eye doctor tells Mrs Patel that she must have an operation.

1   DR: It's a very small operation, Mrs Patel.
2 MARY: It will help your eyes, mother.
        (Begin: *Mary tells her mother . . .*)
3 MRS P: I don't want to have an operation, Mary.
4 MARY: You'll feel much better afterwards, mother.
5 MRS P: My headaches have stopped, doctor.
6   DR: You need this operation, Mrs Patel.
7 MARY: You can't take pills all your life, mother.
8 MRS P: I don't want to go into hospital, Mary.
9   DR: You must try to persuade your mother, Miss Patel.

4 Choose the right endings from the box for these indirect statements:

EXAMPLE
The doctor is sure that Mrs Patel *needs the operation.*

1 The doctor is sure that Mrs Patel . . .
2 But Mary knows that her mother . . .
3 Mary thinks Mrs Patel . . .
4 Mrs Patel knows that her headaches . . .
5 She thinks . . .
6 The doctor hopes that Mary . . .
7 He hopes that Mary will persuade her to . . .
8 But Mary is afraid that . . .

> needs the operation.
> she doesn't need the operation.
> is afraid of hospitals.
> have the operation.
> Mrs Patel will refuse.
> won't agree.
> will explain to her mother.
> have got better.

5 What do you think? Answer, beginning *Yes/No, I think . . .*

EXAMPLE
Will Mrs Patel agree to have the operation?
Yes, I think she will.
OR *No, I think she won't.*
(You decide.)

1 Will Mrs Patel refuse to have the operation?
2 Will her eyes get better without the operation?
3 Will Mary persuade her mother to have the operation?
4 Will Mr Patel persuade her to have it?

Part C Reported and indirect statements with past tense introductory verbs

1 Notice:

> When the introductory verb is in the past tense, there is a change in the tense of the reported verb.
>
> **am/is/are** are reported **was/were**:
> Main verb: 'There's a problem.'
> *He said there was a problem.*
> Auxiliary: 'Your eyes are getting worse.'
> *He said her eyes were getting worse.*
>
> **has/have** are reported **had** (short form **'d**):
> Main verb: 'I have a headache.'
> *She said she had a headache.*
> Auxiliary: 'I've taken a pill.'
> *She said she'd taken a pill.*
> have to: 'I have to ask my boss.'
> *She said she had to ask her boss.*
>
> **will/won't** are reported **would/would not** (short forms **'d/wouldn't**):
> 'I'll phone the hospital.'
> *He said he'd phone the hospital.*
> 'It won't take long.'
> *He told her it wouldn't take long.*
>
> The simple present tense is reported with the simple past tense:
> 'You need an operation.'
> *He said she needed an operation.*
> 'I don't want to.'
> *She said she didn't want to.*
>
> (See Unit 5 for reporting the simple past tense.)

2 Report what the hospital doctor said about Mrs Patel.

EXAMPLE
Her eyes are causing her headaches.
He said her eyes were causing her headaches.

1 She needs an operation.
2 It's very simple.
3 It won't be painful.
4 Her headaches will stop.
5 I know Mrs Patel is afraid.
6 The operation is really necessary.

3 Report these statements with **told** ... **that**:

EXAMPLE
MARY: The operation will help your eyes, mother.
Mary told her mother that the operation would help her eyes.

1 MRS PATEL: I don't want to have an operation, Mary.
2 MRS PATEL: My headaches have stopped, doctor.
3 MARY: The pills have helped your headaches, mother.
4 DOCTOR: Your eyes will be much better after the operation, Mrs Patel.
5 DOCTOR: Your mother really needs this operation, Mary.

4 Notice:

> Report **can/can't** with **could/couldn't**:
> 'I can see.'
> *Mrs Patel said she could see.*
> 'I can't read very well.'
> *She said she couldn't read very well.*
>
> Report **must/mustn't** without any changes:
> 'She must agree.'
> *The doctor said Mrs Patel must agree.*
> 'She mustn't wait.'
> *He said she mustn't wait.*

5 Report **can** and **must**.

EXAMPLE
DOCTOR: You must persuade your mother, Mary.
The doctor said Mary must persuade her mother.

1 MARY: I know I must persuade my mother.
2 MRS PATEL: I can't take time off work.
3 MARY: You must tell your boss about the operation, mother.
4 DOCTOR: I can write to your mother's boss.
5 MRS PATEL: Perhaps I can ask for a holiday.
6 MARY: You mustn't do that, mother.

Part D Reporting the short forms of **is** and **has**; writing practice

1 Notice:

> The short forms of **is** and **has** are the same:
> **'s**.
> She's ready = *She is ready*.
> She's gone = *She has gone*.
>
> To report these correctly, we must know if
> **'s** = **is** or **has** :
> *I told you she was ready*.
> *I told you she'd* (or *she had*) *gone*.

2 Report these statements with **I told you**:

EXAMPLE
It's true.
I told you it was true.

1 It's difficult.
3 She's a librarian.
5 It's impossible.
7 She's found a job.

2 Mary's arrived.
4 She's gone to London.
6 She's looking for a new job.
8 It's a good job.

3 Retell Mrs Patel's story by writing the sentences in each paragraph in the correct order. Begin: *Two weeks ago, . . .*

1 a Two weeks ago, Mary Patel took her mother to the doctor.
  b He gave her some medicine and said she must come back again.
  c Mary told the doctor that her mother got very bad headaches.

2 a Then he told her she must go to the eye hospital.
  b Mrs Patel went back to the doctor last week.
  c He wanted to examine her eyes.

3 a On Wednesday Mrs Patel went to the eye hospital.
  b But Mrs Patel said she didn't want to have the operation.
  c The doctor at the hospital said she had a problem with her eyes.
  d He said that she needed to have a small operation.
  e The doctor told Mary she must persuade her mother.

4 Continue the story by choosing the right words from the box.

Yesterday afternoon Mrs Patel asked her boss for a week's holiday. She didn't explain that she *had* problems with her eyes, and she didn't say that she _1_ an operation. Her boss said he _2_ very sorry, but it _3_ possible.

Mrs Patel came home and told her family that she _4_ have time off. 'So I _5_ have the operation,' she said. 'My boss says it _6_ possible.'

Mary decided that she _7_ go and talk to Mrs Patel's boss. 'I don't think he _8_ ,' she said. 'I _9_ explain about the operation.'

| can't | had | 'll | understands | wasn't |
| couldn't | isn't | needed | was | would |

5 Decide what happened and write the end of the story.

1 Begin the first paragraph: *Mary went and spoke to her mother's boss.*
2 Begin the second paragraph: *When Mary came home, she . . .*
3 Begin the last paragraph: *Finally, Mrs Patel . . .*

UNIT 5 The past perfect

Part A Read and answer

1 Read this passage:

The man who knew too much

At 8.30 this morning the body of a man was found. Someone had murdered him. A small knife was found near the body. The murderer had probably used that knife. The police doctor said the man had died about eight hours before. Therefore the murder had probably happened between midnight and one o'clock.

The police questioned three men. They didn't tell the men about the murder.

The first man said he had been at home the whole evening. He had watched television and gone to bed early.

The second man told the police that he had spent the evening with some friends. They had been to the cinema together. He had got home at about eleven o'clock.

The third man said he didn't know anything about the murder. He told the police, 'I don't know Jim Wilson. I've never owned a knife. I was asleep at midnight. I didn't murder Jim Wilson.'

The police arrested one of the men. Who did they arrest, and why?

2 Find the sentences which answer these questions:

EXAMPLE
How had the man died?
Someone had murdered him.

1 When had the man died?
2 Therefore when had the murder probably happened?
3 Where did the first man say he had been the whole evening?
4 Where had the second man and his friends been?
5 What time had he got home?

3 Complete these sentences:

EXAMPLE
The . . . had probably used . . . .
The murderer had probably used that knife.

1 The . . . had watched television and . . . early.
2 The . . . had spent . . . with . . . .
3 The . . . told the police he had never owned . . . .
4 He said he had been . . . at . . . .
5 He told them he hadn't murdered . . . .

4 Choose the right endings for these sentences about the man who knew too much:

EXAMPLE
The police hadn't talked about the murder, *but one of the men knew about it.*

1 The police hadn't talked about the murder, . . .
2 They hadn't given the time of the murder, . . .
3 They hadn't said the name of the murdered man, . . .
4 They hadn't said anything about the knife, . . .

but one of the men knew about it.
but someone knew it was Jim Wilson.
but someone knew that a knife had been used.
but someone knew it had happened at midnight.

Part B The past perfect in reported and indirect statements

1 Notice:

> The past perfect (**had** + past participle) is used to report the present perfect after a past tense introductory verb (**said,** etc):
> 'I've never owned a knife.' *He said he'd never owned a knife.*

2 Report what the third man said.

EXAMPLE
I haven't seen Jim Wilson for about a month.
He said he hadn't seen Jim Wilson for about a month.

1 I've never known him well.
2 I've never telephoned him.
3 I haven't worked with Wilson.
4 I haven't met his wife.
5 We've never talked about business.
6 Wilson has never borrowed any money from me.

3 Notice:

> We also use the past perfect to report the simple past tense after a past tense introductory verb:
> 'Someone phoned my husband.'
> *She said someone had phoned her husband.*
> 'He was surprised.'
> *She said he had been surprised.*

4 Report what Mrs Wilson told the police.

EXAMPLE
Someone phoned at eleven o'clock.
She told the police that someone had phoned at eleven o'clock.

1 My husband wasn't worried.
2 He didn't tell me the name of the person.
3 He left the house at 11.15.
4 He took a lot of money with him.
5 He told me to go to bed.
6 The same thing happened in September.

5 Notice:

> Remember that the past perfect can report two different tenses: the present perfect, and the simple past tense. We use the simple past tense when we say *when* something happened.

6 Read these reported statements and write the words that the people said:

EXAMPLE
The first man said he had watched television after dinner.
'*I watched television after dinner.*'

1 He told the police he had gone to bed at 10.30.
2 He said he had never met Jim Wilson.
3 The second man said he had met his friends after dinner.
4 He told the police they had left the cinema at 10.15.
5 The third man said he had never owned a knife.
6 He told the police that he hadn't left his house after dinner.

7 Choose the right endings for the third man's sentences. (This is what he finally told the police.)

EXAMPLE
He said he had *phoned Jim Wilson about eleven.*

1 He said he had . . .
2 Wilson had agreed . . .
3 The two men . . .
4 He said they had talked . . .
5 But then an argument . . .
6 He said he had got angry . . .
7 He said he had lied . . .

> phoned Jim Wilson about eleven.
> about some business first.
> and killed Wilson.
> to come and meet him.
> had met each other at 11.30.
> because he had been afraid.
> had started.

Part C Other uses of the past perfect

1 Notice:

> The past perfect is the past-time form of the present perfect:
> *John has found a job.*
> (i.e. he found a job at some time before the present)
> *John had found a job.*
> (i.e. he found a job before a certain time in the past)

2 Rewrite these sentences with the past perfect:

EXAMPLE
The weather has changed.
The weather had changed.

1 It has started to rain.
2 Everyone has gone home.
3 The football match has finished.
4 The players have left.

3 Write sentences with **never** . . . **before.**

EXAMPLE
Peter visited Texas last year.
He had never visited Texas before.

1 He saw an oil well.
2 He met a cowboy.
3 He visited a cattle ranch.
4 He rode a horse.
5 He talked to a millionaire.

4 Write sentences with superlatives and the past perfect.

EXAMPLE
He drove a very large car.
It was the largest car he had ever driven.

1 He ate a very large steak.
2 He saw a very expensive shop.
3 He met some very rich people. (They . . .)

4 He took some very good photographs. (They . . .)
5 He heard some fantastic stories. (They . . .)

5 Notice:

> The past perfect can help us to understand the order of actions or events:
> *We arrived at the station. The train had left.*
> In these sentences, **had left** tells us that this action happened first, before the other action, **arrived.** The meaning is different if we use the simple past tense for both actions:
> *We arrived at the station. The train left.*

6 Decide which sentence is about the earlier action and rewrite it in the past perfect tense with **already.**

EXAMPLE
The rain began at 2.15. I came home at 2.30.
The rain had already begun.

1 I finished my book. Then I went to bed.
2 Mary saw that film in 1982. She didn't want to see it again.
3 Peter went out at seven o'clock. I phoned him about eight.
4 Mrs Patel bought some fruit in the morning. Mary bought some after lunch.

7 Answer the questions and then choose the sentences that are true.

1 When did you go to bed last night? When did you go to sleep?
  a At midnight last night I had already gone to sleep.
  b I was in bed at midnight, but I hadn't gone to sleep.
  c At midnight last night I still hadn't gone to bed.
2 When did you start breakfast this morning? When did you finish?
  a At seven o'clock I'd already started my breakfast.
  b At seven o'clock I'd already finished my breakfast.
  c I hadn't started my breakfast at seven o'clock.

Part D Repeated words; writing practice

1 Notice:

> When words are repeated in sentences like these, we can omit them:
> I went to the post office and I bought some stamps.
> *I went to the post office and bought some stamps.*
>
> He said he'd watched TV and he said he'd gone to bed early.
> *He said he'd watched TV and gone to bed early.*

2 Find the repeated words and write the sentences without them.

EXAMPLE
We stayed at home and we watched television.
We stayed at home and watched television.

1 They made a cup of tea and they went to bed.
2 The second man went out and he met some friends.
3 He said they'd gone to the cinema and they'd seen a film.
4 After the film he'd said goodbye and he'd come home.
5 The third man finally told the police that Wilson had borrowed some money and Wilson hadn't paid it back.
6 He said he had phoned Wilson and he had asked for the money.
7 Wilson had promised to meet him and Wilson had promised to bring the money.

3 Prepare for writing. Answer the questions. (You decide the answers.)

1 What was Jim Wilson's profession?
2 Which town or city did he live in?
3 Where was his body found?
4 What was the date?
5 What is the third man's name?
6 He had lent Wilson some money – how much?
7 The third man wanted to buy something – what?
8 Did he want to threaten Wilson/frighten him/scare him? (Use your dictionary.)

4 Use your answers from Exercise 3 to complete this newspaper report about the murder.

Suspect arrested

The body of Jim Wilson, a (1) who lived in (2), was found (3) on (4). He had been murdered by a man named (5).

At first (5) said he didn't know anything about the murder. He said he didn't know Jim Wilson. The police arrested him, because they thought he knew too much.

Finally (5) told the police this story. Last year Wilson had borrowed (6) from him, and had never paid it back. (5) had decided he needed the money, because he wanted to buy (7). He said he had only wanted to (8) Wilson. He had never intended to kill him. It had all been a terrible mistake.

5 Write a different explanation for the 'terrible mistake'.

Perhaps this *isn't* really the true story: we know that the third man doesn't always tell the truth. Perhaps he planned to murder Wilson. Perhaps Wilson wanted to kill him. Perhaps . . . ? Decide what happened and write a short paragraph.

UNIT 6 Should and ought to

Part A Read and answer

1 Read this passage:

Young People Talk: a television programme

Sally

Ben

SALLY: I work with young people, and I know that they have a lot of problems. Other people don't understand. They say that young people should work harder. They say they earn too much money. These people ought to remember that many young people don't have jobs. They shouldn't forget that jobs are very difficult to find. Unemployment is one of the biggest problems of young people today.

BEN: I think young people should make their own decisions. Other people ought not to decide things for us. I left school when I was sixteen. Perhaps that was a mistake. I haven't found a job yet. Should I go back to school? Should I try to pass my exams now? I don't know. But it's my life, and my problem. I ought to decide.

2 Find the sentences which are similar.

EXAMPLE
They say that young people don't work hard enough.
They say that young people should work harder.

1 People forget that jobs are hard to find.
2 They don't remember that many young people are unemployed.
3 Other people sometimes decide things for us.

3 Complete these sentences with the right words:

EXAMPLE
Ben thinks that __ __ should make their own __.
Ben thinks that young people should make their own decisions.

1 Should Ben try __ __ __ __ now?
2 __ he __ __ to school?
3 Sally says people ought to __ that many __ __ don't have __.
4 They shouldn't __ that __ are __ __ to find.

4 Do you agree or not? Add **I agree** or **I don't agree** at the beginning.

EXAMPLE
. . . that young people should work harder.
I agree that young people should work harder.
OR *I don't agree that young people should work harder.*
(You decide.)

1 . . . that young people should earn less money.
2 . . . that young people should make their own decisions.
3 . . .that Ben ought to decide about his life.

5 Choose a sentence from the box to follow each of these sentences:

EXAMPLE
They say that young people should work harder.
They shouldn't be so lazy.

1 They say that young people should work harder.
2 They say they earn too much money.
3 Other people ought not to decide things for us.
4 I haven't found a job yet.

> They shouldn't be so lazy.
> What should I do?
> They ought to be paid less.
> They should let us decide.

24

Part B Different forms of **should** and **ought to**

1 Notice:

> **Should** and **ought** have the same forms for all persons, singular and plural: **I/you/he should** etc; **I/you/he ought** etc.
>
> The negative forms are **should not** or **shouldn't**; **ought not** or **oughtn't**.
>
> The question forms are **Should I/you/he** etc; **Ought I/you/he** etc.
>
> Notice the form of the verb that follows:
> **should** + infinitive: *They should work harder.*
> **ought** + **to** + infinitive: *They ought to work harder.*

2 Complete with **should** or **ought**.

EXAMPLE
People __ to help each other.
People ought to help each other.

1 They __ try to understand the problems of others.
2 Perhaps older people __ be more helpful.
3 Perhaps young people __ to listen to older people.
4 You __ always listen to advice.
5 You __n't always follow it, of course.
6 You __ to make your own decisions.

3 Complete these opinions about young people with **should** or **shouldn't**. (You decide.)

EXAMPLE
They __ work harder.
They should work harder.

1 They __ talk more politely.
2 They __ earn too much money.
3 They __ try harder to get jobs.
4 They __ be untidy.
5 They __ leave school when they are sixteen.

4 Write sentences with **ought to** and **ought not to** about Ben Hall's brother Sam. Sam is nine.

EXAMPLE
Sam never helps his mother.
He ought to help his mother.

1 Sam never does his homework.
2 He isn't polite to his teachers.
3 He borrows Ben's radio without asking.
4 He never puts the radio back.
5 He hides Ben's shoes.
6 He never says 'please' and 'thank you'.
7 He reads Ben's letters.
8 He never obeys his mother.

5 Notice:

> We report **should** and **ought to** without any changes:
> 'You should say please.'
> *Mrs Hall told Sam he should say please.*
> 'You ought to be more polite.'
> *She said he ought to be more polite.*

6 Report these sentences with **should** and **ought to**:

EXAMPLE
MRS HALL: Sam, you shouldn't do that.
　　　　　(Mrs Hall told Sam)
Mrs Hall told Sam he shouldn't do that.

1 MRS HALL: You ought not to say things like that. (She said)
2 BEN: You should get really angry with Sam, mother. (Ben told his mother)
3 SAM: You should find a job, Ben. (Sam told Ben)
4 BEN: You ought to keep quiet! (Ben said)
5 MRS HALL: Sam, you should get ready for school. (Mrs Hall told Sam)

Part C Using **should** and **ought to** in suggestions and advice

1 Notice:

> In Parts A and B **should** and **ought to** are used to express actions that people think are definitely right or wrong:
> *Young people should work harder.*
> *We ought to make our own decisions.*
>
> We can also use **should** and **ought to** when we are talking about actions that we think are sensible, i.e. to make suggestions or give advice. These sentences are less strong and less definite and often include **perhaps** or **I think** or a question form:
> *Perhaps Ben should join the army.*
> *Perhaps he ought to move to another town.*
> *I think you ought to take the job.*
> *Shouldn't you turn off the electricity first?*

2 What do you advise in these situations? Answer with **I think** . . . **should.**

EXAMPLE
Sally has found a job for Ben. She can tell him now, or she can wait till tomorrow.
I think she should tell him now.
OR *I think she should wait till tomorrow.*
(You decide.)

1 The job is painting Mr Jackson's house. Mr Jackson doesn't like young people. Sally can tell Ben that, or she can keep quiet about it.
2 Ben has never painted a house before. He can accept the job or refuse it.
3 Mr Jackson was a painter when he was young. He can help Ben, or he can say nothing.
4 Ben doesn't know anything about painting. He can ask for help, or he can say he knows all about it.

3 Write Mr Jackson's suggestions, beginning **Shouldn't you** . . .

EXAMPLE
He thinks Ben should move the furniture.
Shouldn't you move the furniture?

1 He thinks Ben should cover the table.

2 He thinks Ben should use a bigger brush.
3 He thinks Ben should move the ladder.
4 He thinks Ben should be more careful.
5 Ben has spilt the paint! Mr Jackson thinks he should say he's sorry.
6 He thinks Ben should clean the floor.

4 Ben has left Mr Jackson's house. Make some suggestions with **Perhaps** . . . **should** or **Perhaps** . . . **ought,** then make some other suggestions of your own.

EXAMPLE
phone Sally.
Perhaps Ben should/ought to phone Sally.

1 go back and apologise.
2 tell Sally he can't do the job.
3 say he'll go back tomorrow.
4 ask someone to help him.

5 Suggest what Mr Jackson should do when someone comes to finish the job. Use the ideas in the box, and add some of your own ideas.

I think	he	should	watch. go into another room. stay in the same room.
I don't think		ought to	go and stay with his sister. be more friendly.

Part D Word study; introductory negatives; writing practice

1 Notice:

> Ben says young people should make their own decisions.
> He thinks other people ought not to decide about his life.
>
> The words **decisions** (a noun) and **decide** (a verb) are related.
> Other examples are:
> **suggest** (verb); **suggestion** (noun)
> **advise** (verb); **advice** (noun)

2 Complete with related words and give the part of speech.

EXAMPLE
Sally is a youth worker. She works with __ people.
Sally is a youth worker. She works with young people. (*adjective*)

1 When a lot of people are unemployed there is a problem of __.
2 Ben and Mr Jackson had an argument. They began to __ when Ben spilt the paint.
3 Many people have difficulties when they look for jobs. Jobs are very __ to find.
4 Ben thinks he should decide about his __ and how he wants to live.
5 Sally informs young people about jobs. She give them __.
6 She advises young people. Her __ is often very helpful.
7 Mr Jackson knows a lot about painting, because he was a __ when he was young.

3 Notice:

> When we introduce a negative indirect statement with **think,** we often move the negative and put it with **think** :
> You shouldn't do that.
> *I don't think you should do that.*
> Ben ought not to argue.
> *I don't think Ben ought to argue.*

4 Rewrite these sentences, beginning **I don't think** . . .

EXAMPLE
Mr Jackson shouldn't be so unfriendly.
I don't think Mr Jackson should be so unfriendly.

1 Ben shouldn't be so careless.
2 Mr Jackson shouldn't shout.
3 He shouldn't show that he dislikes young people.
4 He shouldn't say that everything is wrong.

5 Sally has a problem, too: she can't sleep when she goes to bed. Read about her parents' suggestions.

HER MOTHER: You should go to bed earlier. You stay up too late.
Sally's mother told her that she should go to bed earlier. She said she stayed up too late. Sally tried that, but it didn't help.

HER FATHER: You ought to go for a walk in the evening. The fresh air will make you sleepy.
Her father told her she ought to go for a walk in the evening. He said the fresh air would make her sleepy. Sally tried that, but it didn't help.

6 Continue the story with similar paragraphs about these suggestions, then add another paragraph with your own ideas.

HER BROTHER: You should watch a film on TV. They're so boring that you'll fall asleep at once.

HER SISTER: You ought to do some exercises. They'll help you to relax.

7 Decide what happened and write the end of the story.

Perhaps Sally decided she shouldn't worry. Perhaps she thought she ought to ask her doctor. You decide. Begin the paragraph: *Finally, Sally* . . .

UNIT 7 Relative clauses 1

Part A Read and answer

1 Read this passage:

A strange dream

Last night Tim had a very strange dream.

First he met a man who wanted to sell a house. Tim hadn't met the man before.

After that Tim had to go to the house. The road that went to it was very bad. Tim was in a car, but it wasn't his car. It belonged to the girl who was with him. Tim didn't know her.

They arrived at the house. Suddenly they were in a room which didn't have any doors or windows. (Things that are difficult to understand often happen in dreams!) The only thing that was in the room was an old bicycle.

Then the man who owned the house arrived. Tim gave the man all the money that was in his pocket, and bought the house. But the house was only a pile of stones now.

Tim wanted to ask the man for his money, but the man had gone. He found the bicycle that had been in the house and . . . woke up.

2 Find the clauses that complete these sentences:

EXAMPLE
First he met a man . . .
First he met a man who wanted to sell a house.

1 Suddenly they were in a room . . .
2 Then the man . . . arrived.
3 Tim gave him all the money . . . pocket.
4 He found the bicycle . . . and woke up.

3 Find the sentences with these meanings:

EXAMPLE
A very bad road went to the house.
The road that went to it was very bad.

1 The girl was with Tim. The car belonged to her.
2 Strange things often happen in dreams.
3 One thing was in the room. It was an old bicycle.
4 Then a man arrived. He owned the house.

4 Describe Tim's dream in one paragraph by choosing the right endings from the box.

EXAMPLE
Tim met a man *who wanted to sell a house.*

1 Tim met a man . . .
2 He went to see the house . . .
3 He was in a car . . .
4 The girl who owned the car . . .
5 They went into a room . . .
6 An old bicycle was the only thing . . .
7 The owner of the house arrived . . .
8 He had bought a house . . .

---

who wanted to sell a house.
was with him.
and Tim bought the house from him.
that didn't have any doors!
which was only a pile of stones.
which was for sale.
that was in the room.
that didn't belong to him.

Part B Clauses with subject relative pronouns

1 Notice:

> A subject relative pronoun is a relative pronoun which is the subject of a relative clause.
>
> For people we use the relative pronouns **who** and **that** (**who** is more common):
> *Tim didn't know the girl who was with him.*
> *He gave the money to the man that owned the house.*
>
> For things we use the relative pronouns **that** and **which** (**that** is more common):
> *Tim found the bicycle that had been in the house.*
> *They were in a room which didn't have any doors.*

2 Complete these sentences with **who** or **which**:

EXAMPLE
Tim didn't know the man ＿ was selling the house.
Tim didn't know the man who was selling the house.

1 Tim went to the house ＿ was for sale.
2 He didn't know the girl ＿ was with him.
3 He saw an old bicycle ＿ was in the corner of the room.
4 There are many strange things ＿ only happen in dreams.
5 He saw the man ＿ wanted to sell the house.
6 He gave the money to the man ＿ owned the house.

3 Notice:

> A relative clause must come immediately after the noun it describes:
> *The girl who was with Tim went into the house.*
> (**who was with Tim** describes the girl)
> *The girl went into the house which was for sale.*
> (**which was for sale** describes the house)

4 Add the relative clause in the right place.

EXAMPLE
The road goes to my house. (which turns left)
The road which turns left goes to my house.

1 The books are on the table. (which is near the door)
2 The books are on the table. (that are from the library)
3 You should keep meat in a refrigerator. (which has been cooked)
4 Children often enjoy TV programmes. (that are about animals)
5 Children often want to have a pet. (who like animals)
6 The teacher congratulated the students. (who had passed the exam)
7 The people were glad to see the bus. (who were at the bus stop)

5 Rewrite in one sentence with **who** or **which**:

EXAMPLE
Tim bought a house. It was only a pile of stones.
Tim bought a house which was only a pile of stones.

1 Tim was in a car. It didn't belong to him.
2 He was with the girl. She owned the car.
3 Tim bought the house from the man. The man wanted to sell it.
4 The house was very strange. It was for sale.
5 The man had gone. He sold the house.
6 Tim found the bicycle. It had been in the empty room.

6 Complete this paragraph by choosing the right relative clauses from the box.

A few days later, Tim saw the man *who had been in his dream*. He was someone . .¹. . But he never saw the house . .². , and he never met the girl . .³. . He didn't try to find the road . .⁴. , because it probably didn't exist.

> who had been in his dream
> that led to the house
> who worked in Tim's office
> which had been for sale
> who had gone there with him

Part C Clauses with the possessive relative **whose**

1 Notice:

> We use the possessive relative pronoun **whose** for people and for things. There is a noun after **whose**:
> *Tim met the man whose house was for sale.*
> *That's the woman whose money was stolen.*
> *An equilateral triangle is a triangle whose sides are equal.*
> *Switzerland is a country whose people speak different languages.*

2 Rewrite these sentences without the relative clauses:

EXAMPLE
That's the woman whose money was stolen.
That woman's money was stolen.

1 That's the man whose house is for sale.
2 That's the girl whose mother is Russian.
3 That's the woman whose house is next to the hospital.
4 That's the man whose daughter is in the Olympic team.

3 Rewrite these sentences with **whose** and a relative clause:

EXAMPLE
That man's son plays football for Liverham.
That's the man whose son plays football for Liverham.

1 That woman's husband works in China.
2 That girl's dress cost £200.
3 That man's wife is an actress.
4 That boy's father comes from Yugoslavia.

4 Complete these sentences with **who** or **whose**:

EXAMPLE
Do you know anyone __ name is Mary?
Do you know anyone whose name is Mary?

1 Have you ever met anyone __ works in television?

2 Do you know anyone __ house has twenty rooms?
3 Do you know anyone __ father or mother comes from the United States?
4 Have you ever met anyone __ lives in a house with twenty rooms?
5 Do you know anyone __ job is in television?
6 Do you know anyone __ is called Mary?
7 Have you ever met anyone __ has an American mother or father?

5 Find pairs of sentences in Exercise 4 with similar meanings.

EXAMPLE
Do you know anyone whose name is Mary?
Do you know anyone who is called Mary?

6 Choose one sentence from each pair of sentences in Exercise 5 and answer the question. Use the box to help you.

EXAMPLE
Do you know anyone whose name is Mary?
Yes, I know someone whose name is Mary.
OR *No, I don't know anyone whose name is Mary.*

| Yes, | I know
I've met | someone | who . . . |
|---|---|---|---|
| No, | I don't know
I've never met | anyone | whose . . . |

7 Write true sentences from the box about different fruits and vegetables.

EXAMPLE
An apple *is a fruit whose skin is often eaten.*

1 An apple 2 A banana 3 A lemon
4 An onion 5 A potato 6 A cucumber

| is a | fruit
vegetable | whose skin | is often
is sometimes
is never
isn't often
isn't usually | eaten. |
|---|---|---|---|---|

Now write more sentences about other fruits and vegetables.

Part D The spelling of **who's** and **whose**; writing practice

1 Notice:

> The pronunciation of **who's** (subject relative pronoun + **is** or **has**) and **whose** (possessive relative pronoun) is exactly the same: /huːz/.
> We say and hear the same thing in:
> *The man /huːz/ coming to dinner . . .* and
> *The man /huːz/ son is coming to dinner . . .*
> but we write the word /huːz/ differently:
> *The man who's coming to dinner . . .*
> *The man whose son is coming to dinner . . .*

2 Write these sentences with the correct spelling of /**huːz**/:

EXAMPLE
I don't know the girl /huːz/ sitting in the corner.
I don't know the girl who's sitting in the corner.

1 She's the girl /huːz/ car was stolen.
2 Is she the person /huːz/ worked in China?
3 That's the man /huːz/ picture was in the newspaper.
4 He's the person /huːz/ interested in old books.
5 Yesterday I met someone /huːz/ going to write a book.
6 Do you know anyone /huːz/ eyes are two different colours?

3 Change Tim's dream in Part A Exercise 1 by completing this paragraph:

Tim and a girl went to a house that was for sale. They were in a room which . . . . The only thing that was in the room was . . . . Then . . . Tim wanted to . . . , but . . . . (You decide what finally happened.)

4 Prepare to write a story about a dream. Make short notes.

1 Choose an adjective to describe your dream: frightening/funny/interesting/strange etc.
2 What was the first thing that happened?
3 Where were you?
4 Who were you with? Did you speak to anyone?
5 Who or what did you see?
6 What was the last thing that happened?

5 Describe your dream in two or three paragraphs.

Call your story *A very frightening/funny/ . . . dream*, or think of a different title.

Begin: *A few days ago I had a very . . . dream. This was the first thing that happened. I . . .*

Include some of these relative clauses (remember that strange things can happen in dreams!):

who said he/she was hungry/thirsty/sorry/ . . .
who couldn't speak English/French/ . . .

that didn't belong to me/him/her/them
that wasn't high/long/small/ . . . enough to . . .

which was from my house
which was completely empty

whose face was bright red/green/ . . .
whose eyes were different colours

Finish: *The last thing that happened was this. . . . I was glad/pleased/sorry/sad/ . . . when I woke up, because . . .*

UNIT 8 Relative clauses 2

Part A Read and answer

1 Read this passage:

Madam Zaza explains Tim's dream

TIM: Can you tell me the meaning of the dream I had last week, please?

ZAZA: Perhaps. Tell me about your dream.

TIM: Well, I met a man who wanted to sell a house.

ZAZA: Was he someone you knew?

TIM: No, I didn't know him.

ZAZA: Go on. What happened next?

TIM: I went to the house in a car. The car belonged to the girl that I was with. I didn't know her, either.

ZAZA: Tell me about the house.

TIM: It was very strange. We were in a room that didn't have any doors or windows. Then the man arrived.

ZAZA: The man you had spoken to?

TIM: Yes. I said I'd buy the house. I gave him all the money I had and he left. Then I saw that the house I had bought was only a pile of stones. I had spent all my money on a house that was worth nothing. I found the old bicycle –

ZAZA: Which old bicycle?

TIM : The bicycle that we'd seen in the house. I took it and began to follow the man. Then I woke up. It's one of the strangest dreams I've ever had. Can you explain it?

ZAZA: Oh yes. This is the meaning: you're going to spend a lot of money on something that is completely useless.

TIM : Well, I don't really believe that. Dreams can't really tell us about the future.

ZAZA: Dreams never lie, sir. That will be ten pounds, please.

2 Complete these sentences with the right words:

EXAMPLE
Tim wants to know the __ of the __ he had ____ .
Tim wants to know the meaning of the dream he had last week.

1 The __ belonged to the __ that he was __.
2 Then the __ Tim had spoken to __.
3 Tim found the old __ that they'd __ in the __.
4 It was one of the __ dreams Tim had __ had.

3 Find the sentences that give this information:

EXAMPLE
I was with a girl. The car belonged to her.
The car belonged to the girl that I was with.

1 We were in a room. It didn't have any doors or windows.
2 I gave the man all my money. The man left.
3 I had bought a house. It was only a pile of stones.
4 I had spent all my money. The house was worth nothing.
5 You're going to pay for something. It is completely useless.

Part B Clauses with object relative pronouns

1 Notice:

> An object relative pronoun is a relative pronoun which is the object of a verb or a preposition in a relative clause. (For relative pronouns with prepositions, see Exercise 4 below.)
>
> For people we use the relative pronouns **that** (more common) and **who**. (**Whom** is too formal for conversation and informal writing.):
> *Tim didn't know the man that he met.*
> *The man that Tim saw was the owner of the house.*
>
> For things we use the relative pronouns **that** (more common) and **which**:
> *The house that Tim had bought was a pile of stones.*
> *He took the bicycle that they had seen in the house.*
> (See Part C for contact clauses, i.e. clauses without relative pronouns.)

2 Read these sentences. Explain the meanings.

EXAMPLE
a The books that I bought are on the table.
= *I bought the books.*
b The books are on the table that I bought.
= *I bought the table.*

1 They put the suitcases which they'd borrowed in the car.
2 They put the suitcases in the car which they'd borrowed.
3 He gave the record to the girl that he liked.
4 He gave the record that he liked to the girl.
5 She left the letters which she had received on top of the parcel.
6 She left the letters on top of the parcel which she had received.

3 Write one sentence with a relative clause.

EXAMPLE
Tim was with a girl. He didn't know her.
Tim was with a girl that he didn't know.

1 The man told Tim about a house. He wanted to sell it.
2 The bicycle was very old. They saw it.
3 Tim gave the man the money. He had it in his pocket.
4 He had bought a house. He didn't really want it.
5 Madam Zaza was the name of the fortune teller. Tim asked her about his dream.
6 She gave him an explanation. He didn't like it.

4 Notice the position of relative pronouns with prepositions:

> Prepositions usually come before nouns and pronouns:
> *Tim spoke to the man/to him.*
> *They looked at the house/at it.*
> But in relative clauses the object relative pronoun comes at the beginning of the clause and the preposition comes at the end:
> The man *that Tim spoke to* wanted to sell a house.
> The house *that they looked at* was very odd.

5 Complete these sentences with a relative clause:

EXAMPLE
The house . . . doesn't really exist. (Tim dreamt about the house.)
The house *that Tim dreamt about* doesn't really exist.

1 The car . . . didn't belong to him. (He was in the car.)
2 The house . . . was worth nothing. (He paid for the house.)
3 He didn't know the man . . . (He bought it from the man.)
4 People . . . aren't usually very pleased. (Madam Zaza gets money from people.)

Part C Contact clauses: clauses without object relative pronouns

1 Notice:

> A contact clause is a relative clause which
> leaves out the object relative pronoun:
> *Tim gave the man all the money he had.*
> (= that he had)
> *The man Tim met wanted to sell a house.*
> (= that Tim met)
> *The bicycle they saw was very old.*
> (= that they saw)
> *Tim didn't know the girl he was with.*
> (= that he was with)

2 Add **that** to the contact clauses in these
sentences:

EXAMPLE
I forgot to post the letter I wrote.
I forgot to post the letter that I wrote.

1 The book I'm reading is about aeroplanes.
2 Why didn't you eat the cake I made for you?
3 Go and pay for the things you've chosen.
4 The cat's eating something it found in the
   garden.

3 Rewrite with superlatives and contact clauses.

EXAMPLE
Tim had a strange dream.
It was the strangest dream he had ever had.

1 Kate saw an exciting film.
2 The children watched an interesting TV
   programme.
3 Jane wrote a very long letter.
4 Madam Zaza thought of a clever explanation.

4 Notice:

> Object relative pronouns are the *only* relative
> pronouns that can be left out. Subject and
> possessive relative pronouns can never be left
> out.

5 Rewrite one sentence from each pair using a
contact clause. (It is only possible to use a
contact clause with one sentence in each pair.)

EXAMPLE
a They were in a room that didn't have any doors.
b The room that they were in didn't have any
  doors.
The room they were in didn't have any doors.

1 a Tim gave the man the money that was in his
     pocket.
  b Tim gave the man all the money that he had.
2 a The bicycle that they found was old and dusty.
  b The bicycle that was in the room was old and
     dusty.
3 a The man who owned the house arrived.
  b The man that Tim had spoken to arrived.
4 a Tim had bought a house that he didn't want.
  b Tim had bought a house that was a pile of
     stones.

6 Copy these paragraphs, using contact clauses
where possible:

Madam Zaza is a fortune teller.
Fortune tellers are people who
tell you about the future. The
clothes that they wear are often
very strange.

Some people believe the things
that fortune tellers say, but
others laugh at them. Tim
didn't believe the explanation
that Madam Zaza gave him, but
it came true: he had to pay her
ten pounds. He certainly spent
a lot of money on something
that was quite useless.

7 Go back to Part A Exercise 1 and find three
contact clauses in questions and three contact
clauses in statements.

Part D Punctuation and speaking; review; writing practice

1 Notice:

> In the last unit (Unit 7) and this unit you
> have been learning about defining relative
> clauses, i.e. relative clauses that tell us
> which person or thing is being talked about.
> In speech there is no pause between a noun
> and a relative clause that describes it.
> Write: *The house that Tim bought was a pile*
> *of stones.*
> *He was in a car that didn't belong to*
> *him.*
> Say: *The house that Tim bought was a pile of*
> *stones.*
> *He was in a car that didn't belong to him.*
>
> Practise saying other sentences with defining
> relative clauses from this unit and Unit 7.

2 Review of relative pronouns that are used in
defining relative clauses:

> Unit 7 and this unit have practised these
> relative pronouns (∅ = no relative pronoun:
> you can use a contact clause):
>
> | | SUBJECT | POSSESSIVE | OBJECT |
> |---|---|---|---|
> | PEOPLE | who/that | whose | that/who/∅ |
> | THINGS | that/which | whose | that/which/∅ |

3 Ask Madam Zaza to explain a dream you have
really had. Begin like this:

(NAME): *Can you explain a dream I had, please?*
ZAZA: *Yes, I'll try. What happened in your dream?*
(NAME): ...
ZAZA: *I see. Go on, please.*

Decide how to write the middle of the
conversation. Then finish:

(NAME): *What does it mean? Do you know?*
ZAZA: *Oh yes, that's quite easy. It means ...*
(NAME): ...

4 Prepare for writing:

1 Name a country that you would like to visit.
2 Name a country that you don't want to visit.
3 Name a country that you would like to study in.
4 Name a country that you would like to work in.
5 Name a city in one of these countries.

5 Write a short paragraph about each country.
You can add your own ideas, too.

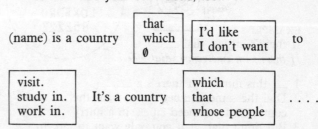

(name) is a country | that which ∅ | I'd like I don't want | to

visit. study in. work in. | It's a country | which that whose people | . . . .

6 Choose a title, and write a paragraph about it:

The most interesting thing that has happened to me this
year
OR *The best meal/worst meal that I've ever eaten*

Your paragraph should answer some of these
questions: What? Where? When? Who? How?
Why?

UNIT 9 Conditional clauses 1

Part A Look, read and answer

1 Look at the information in the picture and find the right words to complete these sentences about emergency telephone calls:

FIRE
DIAL POLICE
999 AMBULANCE

LOXFORD
852222

EXAMPLE
If there's an ___, dial ___.
If there's an emergency, dial 999.

1 ___ this number if there's a ___.
2 Dial the same number if you want the ___ to come, or if you need an ___ in a hurry.
3 But don't dial ___ if you only want to talk to your friend.
4 Dial 999 for ___ telephone ___ only.

2 Use the words in the box to complete the sentences about water.

Water
boiling point 100° centigrade → steam
freezing point 0° centigrade → ice

freezes	heat	heated
ice	steam	water

EXAMPLE
If you ___ water it boils at 100°C.
If you heat water, it boils at 100°C

1 It ___ at 0°C if it is cooled.
2 Water changes into ___ if you boil it.
3 Steam changes into ___ if you cool it.
4 If water is cooled, it changes into ___.
5 Ice changes into water if it is ___.

3 Choose the right endings from the box to complete these sentences about the postman.

EXAMPLE
If the postman goes into the garden, *the dog will probably bite him.*

1 If the postman goes into the garden, . . .
2 If he doesn't go in, . . .
3 But he'll have to go in . . .
4 If there aren't any letters, . . .
5 The postman will be pleased . . .

the dog will probably bite him.
if he has some letters for that house.
he'll be all right.
if he doesn't have to go in.
he won't have to go in.

4 Use the words in the box to complete the sentences about Tom and his mother.

Tom! Don't jump on that chair! Get down at once or I'll be angry. I'll send you to bed if you don't stop!

does	she's	stops	doesn't	gets
she'll	will	send	stop	won't

EXAMPLE
Tom's mother ___ be angry if Tom ___ get down.
Tom's mother will be angry if Tom doesn't get down.

1 But if he ___ down she ___ be angry.
2 She says ___ send him to bed if he doesn't ___.
3 Of course she won't ___ him to bed if he ___ now.
4 ___ often angry when Tom ___ things like that.

36

Part B Sentences with *if* with the present tense in each clause

1 Notice:

> Statements about general truth, or about something which happens regularly, have the present tense in both clauses:
> *If you heat water, it boils.*
> *If it rains, I go to work by bus.*
>
> We can use **when** in these sentences without changing the meaning:
> *When you heat water, it boils.*
> *When it rains, I go to work by bus.*
>
> The **if** clauses can come first or second:
> *If it's sunny, I walk to work.*
> *I walk to work if it's sunny.*
> There is often a comma after the **if** clause when it comes first.

2 Rewrite these sentences, beginning with **If**:

EXAMPLE
Water which is cooled to 0°C freezes.
If water is cooled to 0°C, it freezes.

1 Steam which meets something cold changes into water.
2 Children who are happy usually behave well.
3 People who work hard are often successful.
4 Animals that are looked after well are usually healthy.

3 Complete these sentences. Use your own ideas.

EXAMPLE
If the weather is very warm, I often . . .
If the weather is very warm, I often go swimming.

1 If the weather is very warm, I often . . . .
2 But I never . . . if it's cold.
3 If it's raining, I usually . . . .
4 If the weather's good at the weekend, I sometimes . . . .
5 I always feel happy if . . . .

4 Rewrite these general statements in one sentence with **If**:

EXAMPLE
Tom often jumps on the furniture. His mother gets angry.
If Tom jumps on the furniture, his mother gets angry.

1 She usually sees him. She tells him to stop.
2 She often gets really angry. She sends him to bed.
3 But Tom usually promises to be good. She says he can get up.
4 Sometimes Tom is very naughty. His mother tells his father.

5 Decide what usually happens and complete these sentences:

EXAMPLE
If Tom doesn't behave well at school, . . .
If Tom doesn't behave well at school his teacher tells his mother.
OR . . . *his teacher sends him to the headmaster.*
(You decide.)

1 If Tom takes his sister's toys, . . .
2 If Tom isn't polite to people, . . .
3 If Tom behaves very well, . . .
4 If Tom wants something, . . .

Part C First conditional: sentences with **if** about the present or the future

1 Notice:

These sentences are about particular events
or actions which are possible now or in the
future: perhaps they will happen and
perhaps they won't happen. We use the
present tense in the **if** clause and **will/won't**
in the main clause:
*If Tom jumps on the chair again, his mother
will be angry.*
*If he doesn't stop at once, she'll send him to
bed.*

Notice the difference between these two
sentences:
If it's sunny tomorrow, I'll walk to work.
(statement about a particular time and
event/action)
If it's sunny, I walk to work.
(general statement as in Part B)

2 Complete the sentences with the right forms of
the verbs.

EXAMPLE
If the postman ⎯ into the garden, the dog ⎯
him. (go, bite)
*If the postman goes into the garden, the dog will bite
him.*

1 If the dog ⎯ him, the postman ⎯ any more
  letters to that house. (bite, not take)
2 So if the people in the house ⎯ to get their
  letters, they ⎯ to keep the dog inside.
  (want, have)
3 But perhaps naughty children ⎯ into the garden
  if the dog ⎯ there. (go, not be)
4 If they ⎯ in, perhaps they ⎯ the bell and run
  away. (go, ring)
5 Perhaps someone ⎯ them if they ⎯ fast
  enough. (catch, not run away)
6 If someone ⎯ the children, perhaps they ⎯ it
  again. (catch, not do)

3 Complete the **if** clauses to make sensible
sentences. (You decide.)

EXAMPLE
I'll be very surprised if . . . tomorrow.
I'll be very surprised if I get ten letters tomorrow.

1 No one will be surprised if . . . tomorrow.
2 If . . . , I'll be very pleased.
3 I'll have a good time at the weekend if . . . .
4 If . . . , I'll work harder next year.
5 I'll go to the cinema if . . . on Friday.

4 Write conditional sentences about these
possible events. What will you do?

EXAMPLE
Perhaps it'll rain tomorrow.
If it rains, I'll stay at home.

1 Perhaps there will be a good film on TV tonight.
2 Perhaps you'll be hungry at midnight.
3 Perhaps you'll be late for school/work tomorrow.
4 Perhaps there will be a lot of snow next winter.

5 Rewrite with the **if** clause second:

Help me, or
I'll fall.

EXAMPLE
Help me, or I'll fall.
I'll fall if you don't help me.

1 Write it down, or you'll forget it.
2 Hurry, or we'll miss the bus.
3 Stop it, or I'll go away.
4 Be careful, or you'll drop it.
5 Have a sandwich now, or you'll be hungry later.
6 Go to bed, or you'll be very tired tomorrow.
7 Drive faster, or we'll be late.
8 Tell me the answer, or I'll never finish my
  homework.

Part D Short verb forms in conditional sentences; writing practice

1 Notice these short verb forms in conditional sentences:

Verbs like **be** and **can** :
Are you ready? *If you are, we'll leave.*
(= if you are ready)
If you aren't, we'll wait.
(= if you aren't ready)
Other verbs need **do**:
I hope he *If he does, he'll tell us.*
knows. (= if he knows)
If he doesn't, we'll tell him.
(= if he doesn't know)
Do you like it? *If you do, I'll buy it.*
(= if you like it)
*If you don't, we'll go to
another shop.*
(= if you don't like it)
Will she come? *If she does I'll be glad.*
(= if she comes)
If she doesn't, I'll be sorry.
(= if she doesn't come)

2 Complete with the right short verb forms:

EXAMPLE
Jane hopes her exams are easy. If they ___, she'll pass. If they ___ she'll probably fail.
Jane hopes her exams are easy. If they are, she'll pass. If they aren't, she'll probably fail.

1 Can you swim? If you ___, we'll swim to the island. If you ___, I'll teach you.
2 Do you know Mary? If you ___, I'll introduce you. But if you ___, then I won't need to.
3 Do they understand French? If they ___, they'll enjoy that French film. But if they ___, they'll be bored.
4 Will Aunt Florence like her birthday present? If she ___, she'll write and thank us. But if she ___, she won't say anything.
5 Will Liverham win their football match? They'll win the cup if they ___, and if they ___, everyone will be disappointed.

3 Write two paragraphs to a friend who is coming to visit your country. The first paragraph is general advice, and the second paragraph is about meeting your friend.

Paragraph one

If you come to (country) in (month), { you should / bring some / don't bring any }

{ warm / summer } clothes, because it will be { very / quite } { hot / warm / cool / cold }

then. But { remember to bring / you ought to bring } ... if you { want / plan / intend }

to go to { the coast. / the mountains. / .... } If you want to take a lot

of photographs, { bring some films with you. / wait, and buy films here. }

They're { very / quite } { cheap / expensive } in (country).

Paragraph two

If you come { by plane / by train } and arrive

{ at the weekend, / on Saturday or Sunday, } I'll come and meet you at

the { airport. / station. } But if you arrive { before lunchtime / before ... o'clock }

on a weekday, you'll have to { take a taxi, / get the bus, } because

I'll be at { school / work } then.

4 Write two paragraphs about what you will do next weekend. Complete the opening sentence of each paragraph, and then write one or two sentences about your plans.

Begin the first paragraph:
If the weather is good next weekend, I'll ...
Begin the second paragraph:
If the weather isn't very good, I'll probably ...

UNIT 10 The past progressive

Part A Read and answer

1 Read this passage:

One famous actress remembers another

Carol Ravenna is a film actress who has made
several animal films. She is talking about an
elephant called Hekima.
'I met Hekima for the first time when I went to
Africa five years ago. We were in Tanzania, and we
were making a film about elephants.
When we arrived we saw three young elephants.
They were playing together. Hekima was the
smallest, and the friendliest. She was also very
intelligent. That was why we called her Hekima: it
means wisdom. Hekima was a marvellous actress,
and the film made her famous.
After we'd finished the film we left Africa, of
course. I thought: "I'll never see Hekima again."
But she left Africa, too. She came to a zoo in
England. I was working in America when I heard
about that. Two months later I went to see
Hekima. She seemed to be happy when I saw her.
She was playing in her usual way. I think she
remembered me.'

2 Find the right words to complete the sentences.

EXAMPLE
Carol __ Hekima when she __ to Africa __ __ ago.
Carol met Hekima when she went to Africa five years ago.

1 They __ in Tanzania, and they __ __ a film
  about __.
2 When they __ they saw __ __ __.
3 They were __ together.
4 Carol __ __ in America when she __ that
  Hekima was in a __ in __.
5 Hekima __ to be happy when Carol __ her.
6 She __ __ in her __ way.

3 Complete the sentences by choosing the right
   endings from the box:

EXAMPLE
About five years ago, a film company *was making a
film in Tanzania.*

1 About five years ago, a film company . . .
2 Carol Ravenna . . .
3 Three young elephants . . .
4 When Carol arrived, the elephants . . .
5 Someone . . .
6 One of the elephants . . .

was making a film in Tanzania.
were acting in it, too.
were playing together in a river.
was acting in the film.
was throwing water at the others.
was teaching them to act.

4 Use the words in the box to continue Carol's
   story.

enjoying look playing saw unhappy working

Last year I was *working* in England. I visited
Hekima again. When I __1__ her, she wasn't __2__ in
her usual way. She didn't __3__ at me. Poor Hekima!
She wasn't __4__ her life at the zoo. I knew that she
was very, very __5__ .

Part B Form and use of the past progressive

1 Notice:

> We form all progressive tenses with parts of **be** and a present participle. The past progressive, therefore, is formed with **was/were + -ing**:
> *We were making a film in Africa.*
> *Hekima was standing in a corner.*
> *She wasn't doing anything.*
> The past progressive is the past-time form of the present progressive:
> We're making a film.
> *She said they were making a film.*
> I'm doing my homework.
> *I was doing my homework at this time yesterday.*
> The past progressive can describe actions or events which continued for some time or which were repeated a number of times:
> *It was raining, and we were getting very wet.*
> *The elephants were playing in the river.*
> *The children were laughing and shouting.*

2 Rewrite using the past progressive.

EXAMPLE
Carol's working in America.
Carol was working in America.

1 She's acting in a play.
2 Hekima is playing with another elephant.
3 They're standing in the river.
4 Some people are watching them.
5 The elephants aren't looking at the people.
6 One of the men is listening to his radio.

3 Notice:

> We use the simple past, not the past progressive, of **be** in sentences like these:
> *They were in Africa.*
> *Hekima was very unhappy.*
> We use the simple past, not the past progressive, of **have** in sentences like these:
> *They had a big house near the park.*
> *Carol had a good idea.*
> But when **have** has a special meaning, we can use the past progressive:
> *They were having lunch. (have = eat)*
> *I was having a cup of coffee in the kitchen.*
> *(have = drink)*
> Some other verbs which are not normally used in the past progressive are: **call** (= give a name), **know, like, see** and **seem**.

4 Complete these sentences with the right form of **be** or **have.**

EXAMPLE
Carol Ravenna __ in Africa five years ago. (be)
Carol Ravenna was in Africa five years ago.

1 One day Hekima ran away while everyone __ lunch. (have)
2 The director __ very worried. (be)
3 Then he __ a good idea. (have)
4 There __ two old cameras that nobody used any more. (be)
5 He knew Hekima __ very interested in cameras. (be)
6 While everyone __ coffee, he put them outside the camp. (have)
7 It __ a very good idea, because Hekima came back very soon. (be)

5 Answer the questions and write a true paragraph.

EXAMPLE
It's eleven o'clock now. Yesterday at this time I was at school. I was learning history.

1 What time is it now? Yesterday at this time, where were you?
2 What were you doing?
3 Where were other people in your family? What were they doing?

Part C The past progressive in sentences with **when** and **while**

1 Notice:

> The past progressive can help us to understand the time relationship between actions or events. These sentences show that one action or event started and was continuing, and then another action or event happened:
> *Carol was working in America when she heard about Hekima.*
> *When the phone rang, I was watching television.*
> The actions of **working** and **watching** began first, before the other things happened, and perhaps continued after they had happened.

2 Complete the sentences with the right past tenses.

EXAMPLE
When Carol ___, the young elephants ___ together. (arrive, play)
When Carol arrived, the young elephants were playing together.

1 Carol ___ in Hollywood when she ___ that Hekima was in England. (work, hear)
2 When Carol ___ Hekima the first time, she ___ happily. (visit, play)
3 But Hekima ___ anything when Carol ___ to the zoo last month. (not do, go)
4 She ___ in a corner when Carol ___. (stand, arrive)
5 Carol ___ in her living room one evening when she ___ the phone. (sit, hear)

3 Notice:

> We often use **while** to start a clause with the past progressive verb:
> *Carol met Hekima while she was making a film.*
> *Hekima became dangerous while she was living in the zoo.*

4 Choose a **while** clause from the box to rewrite the endings.

EXAMPLE
Carol and her husband talked about Hekima at dinner.
Carol and her husband talked about Hekima *while they were having dinner*.

1 Carol and her husband talked about Hekima at dinner.
2 Carol suddenly felt very unhappy during the conversation.
3 She was still thinking about Hekima when she made some coffee.
4 Her husband told her to go and have her coffee. 'I'll wash the dishes,' he said.
5 Carol turned the TV on before she finished her coffee.
6 The phone rang in the middle of the programme.

while	he she they	was were	having dinner. making some coffee. watching the programme. washing the dishes. discussing Hekima. drinking her coffee.

5 Write the end of Carol's story about Hekima by choosing the right endings from the box.

EXAMPLE
After I'd visited Hekima, *I really began to worry about her.*

1 After I'd visited Hekima . . .
2 Then, on Monday, we heard . . .
3 Someone phoned from the zoo . . .
4 My husband . . .
5 When I saw his face . . .
6 'Hekima died this morning,' . . .

> I really began to worry about her.
> while I was watching television.
> he said sadly.
> answered the telephone.
> that Hekima had died.
> I knew that he had some bad news.

Part D Punctuation: exclamation marks and colons; writing practice

1 Notice:

An exclamation mark (!) shows strong feelings of surprise, excitement, sorrow, etc:
Hekima began to attack one of the keepers!
She was very unhappy. Poor Hekima!
Strong commands can have exclamation marks:
Hurry! You must be quick!
But these are reported without the exclamation mark:
She said he must be quick.
A colon (:) is often used before a list, explanation or example:
Hekima wasn't doing anything: she wasn't eating, she wasn't . . .
We called her Hekima: it means wisdom.
The keeper said Hekima was dangerous: she had attacked him twice.

2 Add exclamation marks, colons or full stops to these sentences:

EXAMPLE
Carol said, 'Hekima has taken my handbag'
Carol said, 'Hekima has taken my handbag!'

1 She told the director Hekima had taken her handbag
2 He answered angrily, 'Forget about it'
3 Carol was in two films with Hekima 'Elephants' and 'Jungle Story'
4 She likes elephants and she hates lions, but she also made a film with ten lions
5 Carol will always remember two things about Hekima her friendliness and her intelligence
6 The keepers at the zoo will only remember Hekima's problems she became wild and dangerous, and she attacked people
7 After Hekima's death, Carol felt that she had lost a friend Poor Carol

3 Write a story about one of the funny things Hekima did while the film was being made. Choose how to start and continue the story.

One {day / afternoon} Carol was very {tired, / sleepy,} because she had got up {at . . . o'clock. / very early.} She was {sleeping / resting} in her tent when suddenly {she heard / there was} a {very loud / tremendous} noise. Carol {got up / ran out of the tent} {at once / quickly} and saw the reason: Hekima was {standing on . . . / sitting on . . . / trying to . . .} Then, while Carol was watching her, she . . .

4 Write a paragraph describing how Hekima attacked one of the keepers at the zoo. Pretend you are the keeper who was attacked.

Begin: *Hekima was drinking some water when I went in to clean her cage.*
Finish: *I'm not really sorry that she died. I was always frightened of her after she'd attacked me. We all thought she was going to kill someone.*

UNIT 11 Reported and indirect questions 1

Part A Read and answer

1 Read this passage:

An interview for a job

Liz Black is interviewing Ron Harris for a job as a salesman.

LIZ: Please sit down, Mr Harris. I have your application form here, so I know how old you are, and I know about your education and your other jobs. I know where you work now. Why are you looking for a new job, Mr Harris? Don't you like your present job?

RON: Oh yes, I'm quite happy, but . . .

LIZ: Well, why do you want this job? Are you interested in selling things?

RON: It's a better job, and I think I'd enjoy it. I'd like to be a salesman.

LIZ: How did you hear about the job? Did you see an advertisement?

RON: No, someone told me about it.

LIZ: Who told you? Was it Jack Baker?

RON: Yes, that's right. How did you know?

LIZ: Oh, he said something about you last week. What did he say about his work? Does he enjoy it?

RON: Very much.

2 Complete with **asks** or **doesn't ask**:

EXAMPLE
Liz __ Ron why he wants this job.
Liz asks Ron why he wants this job.

1 She __ why he's looking for a new job.
2 She __ what age he is.
3 She __ where he went to school, either.
4 She __ how he heard about the job.
5 She __ who told him about it.
6 She __ which other jobs he has had.

3 Find the right words to complete the sentences.

EXAMPLE
__ asks __ why he wants a new __.
Liz asks Ron why he wants a new job.

1 She asks if he's __ in selling __.
2 She asks if Ron saw an __ for the job.
3 She wants to know if __ told __ about the job.
4 __ asks __ how she knew that.
5 She asks him what __ said about his __.

4 Find the questions that go before or after these questions:

EXAMPLE
Don't you like your present job?
Why are you looking for a new job, Mr Harris?
Don't you like your present job?

1 How did you hear about the job?
2 Are you interested in selling things?
3 Who told you?   4 Does he enjoy it?

5 Choose the right questions from the box to follow these questions:

EXAMPLE
When can you start? *Soon?*

1 When can you start?
2 How long must you stay in your present job?
3 Where do you live?
4 Which part of the city do you live in?
5 What about your wife's work?

Soon?   Until next month?   In London?
Does she have a good job?   The centre?

Part B Reported questions with question words: present tense introductory verbs

1 Notice:

DIRECT QUESTIONS	REPORTED QUESTIONS
Where is my book?	*I want to know where my book is.*
When can Ron start work?	*Liz asks when Ron can start work.*
Why has he gone?	*She wants to know why he has gone.*
Where does Ron live?	*I don't know where Ron lives.*

Look at the structure of the reported questions:

introduction + question word + subject + verb + . . .

I don't know   where   Ron   lives.

Notice that reported questions have the same order as statements (subject + verb), and that forms of auxiliary **do** are not needed.

2 Complete these two lists:

DIRECT QUESTIONS	INDIRECT QUESTIONS
1 *When is he coming?*	*I don't know when he is coming.*
2 Where are they going?	I want to know . . .
3 . . .	I wonder how much Ron earns.
4 Why does she love him?	No one knows . . .
5 . . .	I wonder how long Jack has worked there.
6 How does Jack like his job?	Liz asks . . .

3 Notice:

Pronouns, verb persons and possessive adjectives are changed in reported questions in the same ways as in reported statements:

What do you think?	*She asks what he thinks.*
Where is my coat?	*He wants to know where his coat is.*

After a present tense introductory verb the verb tense is not changed.

4 Report these questions.
   Begin: *Liz asks Ron . . .*

EXAMPLE
Why do you want a new job?
Liz asks Ron why he wants a new job.

1 How many hours do you work every week?
2 What is your salary?
3 How long have you had your present job?
4 Where does your wife work?
5 Which parts of the country do you know?
6 When can you start working for us?

5 Notice:

There are two kinds of direct questions with **who**:
1 Who saw you? (= someone saw you; **who** is the subject of **saw**)
2 Who did you see? (= you saw someone; **who** is the object of **see**)
Notice how we report these questions:
1 *I want to know who saw you.* (same order as direct question when **who** is the subject)
2 *I want to know who you saw.* (order is question word + subject + verb)

6 Write direct questions from these reported questions:

EXAMPLE
Ron's wife asks who he spoke to.
Who did you speak to?

1 She asks who spoke to him.
2 She asks who he met.
3 She asks who was most helpful.
4 She asks who he will work with.

Part C Reported questions with question words: past tense introductory verbs

1 Notice:

> When we use a past tense introductory verb (**asked** etc) to report a question, the tense of the verb must be changed in the same way as in reported statements:
>
> | | |
> |---|---|
> | 'Why do you want the job?' | *She asked me why I wanted the job.* |
> | 'Why are you looking for a new job?' | *She asked me why I was looking for a new job.* |
> | 'How did you hear about it?' | *She asked me how I had heard about it.* |
> | 'Which parts of England have you worked in?' | *She asked me which parts of England I had worked in.* |
> | 'What will your wife say?' | *She asked me what you would say.* |

2 Read what Ron told his wife about the interview, and then write down the direct questions that Liz Black asked Ron in the interview.

She didn't ask me which other jobs I had had, but she wanted to know how long I had been in my present job. She asked why I was looking for a new job, and how I had heard about the job. She wanted to know when I could start and how my wife would feel about moving to another city.

EXAMPLE
How long . . .?
How long have you been in your present job?

1 Why . . .?	2 How . . .?
3 When . . .?	4 How . . .?

3 Report the questions that Ron's wife asked about the future. Begin: *She asked him . . .*

EXAMPLE
When will you start?
She asked him when he would start.

1 What will you say to your boss?
2 How much are they going to pay you?
3 Where will we have to live?

4 How am I going to find a job?
5 What will a new house cost?

4 Choose the right question words from the box to complete these reported questions:

EXAMPLE
Ron's wife wanted to know __ the company was.
Ron's wife wanted to know how big the company was.

1 She asked him __ salesmen there were.
2 She wondered __ he would be paid.
3 She wanted to know __ he would have to start work in the morning.
4 Then she asked __ Liz Black was.
5 She wondered __ Liz had worked for the company.

how big	how many	how old
how long	how much	what time

5 Write a dialogue between Ron and his wife (her name is Sandra), using her questions from Exercise 4. Decide how Ron answers each question.

EXAMPLE
SANDRA: *How big is the company?*
  RON: *Not very big. About forty people work for it./Quite big. It employs 300 people./Very big. It's an international company./I don't know./I'm not sure./I didn't ask.*

6 Report your dialogue from Exercise 4 with indirect questions and indirect statements. Use **asked, asked him/Ron, wanted to know** for questions; and **said, told her/Sandra, answered that** for statements.

EXAMPLE
When Sandra asked how big the company was, Ron told her it wasn't very big. He said about forty people worked for it.

Part D Punctuation in reported and indirect questions; writing practice

1 Notice:

Direct questions finish with a question mark:
Where's Ron?
We can report this question in a statement:
I want to know where Ron is.
It can also be reported in a question:
Do you know where Ron is?
The form of the introductory verb tells us which punctuation mark to use. **I want to know** is a statement, and needs a full stop; **Do you know** is a question, and needs a question mark.
The same thing is true about reported and indirect statements:
I think he's in the garden.
(**I think** is a statement.)
Do you think he's in the garden?
(**Do you think** is a question.)

2 Copy these sentences, underlining the introductory verb phrase and putting a full stop or a question mark at the end.

EXAMPLE
Do you know which cinema is showing 'Son of Superman'
Do you know which cinema is showing 'Son of Superman'?

1 Did someone say it was the Odeon
2 No one told me where it was
3 Jane could tell us, but I don't know where she is
4 She's gone out, but she didn't say where she was going
5 Well, did she tell you when she'd get back
6 No, she didn't. I wonder when the film starts

3 Write six true sentences from the box, putting the answer at the end if you know it.

EXAMPLE
I know who discovered America: (name).
OR *I can't remember who discovered America.*

I know	who	discovered America.
I don't know	where	a football match lasts.
I'm not sure	when	Timbuktu is.
I can't	what	the first moon
remember	how long	landing was.
	which	has the most speakers.
	language	the capital of Finland is.

4 Write six questions that you can answer about history, geography, general knowledge, etc.

EXAMPLE
Who is the president of the United States?

1 Who . . .? 2 What . . .? 3 Where . . .?
4 When . . .? 5 How long . . .? 6 How much/
                                      many . . .?

5 Ask a number of people your questions from Exercise 4 and note their answers: correct or incorrect/don't know. Then change things in the paragraphs below to make them a true description of your questions and answers.

Paragraph 1: *I asked (five) people these questions:*
1 Who is the president of the United States?
2 What . . . .? (etc)
The total number of questions was (thirty), and there were (nineteen) correct answers.

Paragraph 2: *Everyone knew who the president of the United States was. (Three) of them knew what . . . (No one) knew where . . . . (etc)*

Paragraph 3: *The easiest question was question (one) with (five) correct answers and the most difficult questions were question (three) with (no) correct answers and question (six) with (one) correct answer.*

Paragraph 4: *Here are the correct answers:*
1 (name) is the president of the United States. (etc)

UNIT 12 Reported and indirect questions 2

Part A Read and answer

1 Read this passage:

Judy wants to go to Rome

Judy is in a travel agency. She wants to know about different ways of going to Rome.

ERIC: Can I help you?
JUDY: Yes please. I want to know about fares to Rome.
ERIC: How do you want to go? By air? By train?
JUDY: It depends on the price. Is the return air fare very expensive?
ERIC: Well, that depends on several things. When do you want to go? Next week? Next month? When?
JUDY: In the summer, probably in July.
ERIC: How long are you going to stay there? More than a month?
JUDY: No, only two or three weeks.
ERIC: And are you going to book the ticket now?
JUDY: Yes, probably.
ERIC: Right. The fare will be £172.
JUDY: Is that the cheapest fare?
ERIC: It's the cheapest air fare in July, yes.
JUDY: Oh. Is it cheaper by train, then?

2 Find the right words to complete the sentences.

EXAMPLE
Eric asks if Judy wants to go to Rome by __ or by __.
Eric asks if Judy wants to go to Rome by air or by train.

1 Judy wants to know if the return __ __ is very __.
2 He asks if she __ to go next __ or next __ or some other time.
3 Then he asks if she is going to __ there more than a __.
4 He wants to know if she is __ to book the __ now.
5 Judy asks him if £172 is the __ fare.
6 Finally she wants to know if it's __ by __.

3 Complete these sentences with **asks** or **doesn't ask**:

EXAMPLE
Eric __ Judy why she wants to go to Rome.
Eric doesn't ask Judy why she wants to go to Rome.

1 He __ how she wants to go.
2 Judy __ if the return air fare is very expensive.
3 She __ which airlines fly to Rome.
4 He __ when she wants to go.
5 Judy __ if £172 is the cheapest air fare.
6 She __ if it's possible to go to Rome by bus.

4 Choose the right endings from the box for the things Judy told her sister that evening.

EXAMPLE
I asked if it was cheaper *by train.*

1 I asked if it was cheaper . . .
2 I wanted to know how much . . .
3 Then I asked how long the . . .
4 I wanted to know if I had to . . .
5 Then I asked if I needed . . .

by train	to book a seat now.
train journey took.	change trains.
the train fare was.	

Part B Reported **yes/no** questions: present tense introductory verb

1 Notice:

> We report **yes/no** questions (i.e. questions that do not have a question word) with **if** :
> Are they ready?   *I'll ask if they're ready.*
> Does she like it?   *He wants to know if she likes it.*
>
> Notice that reported questions have the same order as statements (subject + verb + . . .) and that forms of auxiliary **do** are not needed.
>
> We make the same changes with pronouns, verb persons and possessive adjectives as in other reported sentences. After a present tense introductory verb the tense of the verb is not changed.

4 Notice:

> We can use **whether** instead of **if** in reported questions:
> I'll ask **whether** they're ready.
> He wants to know **whether** she likes it.
> (We practise **if** in sentences like these because it is more common.)
>
> We often prefer to use **whether** in sentences that include **or** :
>
> 'Do you want to go by air or by train?'   *Eric asks Judy whether she wants to go by air or by train.*
>
> 'Are you going to pay now or later?'   *He wants to know whether she's going to pay now or later.*

2 Complete these two lists:

DIRECT QUESTIONS	INDIRECT QUESTIONS
1 *Will Judy go by plane?*	*I wonder if Judy will go by plane.*
2 Will she go by train	I wonder . . .
3 . . .	I don't know if she can afford £172.
4 Does she like flying?	I'll ask her . . .
5 . . .	I wonder if she's going to stay in a hotel.
6 Does she know anyone in Rome?	Ask her . . .
7 . . .	I wonder if she's going alone.

3 Write questions.
Begin: *Do you know* . . .

EXAMPLE
Does Judy speak Italian?
Do you know if Judy speaks Italian?

1 Does Judy speak any foreign languages?
2 Has she been to Italy before?
3 Can she stay with her friends in Rome?
4 Is she going with her sister?
5 Do Judy and her sister like Italian food?
6 Will Judy have to get a new passport?

5 Report these questions using **whether** . . . **or**.
Begin: *Eric asks Judy whether* . . .

EXAMPLE
When do you want to go? Now or in the summer?
Eric asks Judy whether she wants to go now or in the summer.

1 How long will you stay? Less than a month or more than a month?
2 Which day do you want to leave? On the fourth or the fifth?
3 Are you going to travel first class or not?
4 When do you want to pay? Today or when you get the ticket?
5 How are you going to pay? By cheque or in cash? (cash = money)

6 Decide how to complete these sentences:

EXAMPLE
Our English teacher sometimes asks us if . . .
Our English teacher sometimes asks us if we understand everything.
OR . . . *we want to play a game in English*

1 Our English teacher often asks us if . . . but he/she never asks us if . . .
2 I sometimes ask him/her if . . .
3 At home, I sometimes ask my mother/father if . . .

Part C Reported **yes/no** questions: past tense introductory verbs

1 Notice:

> After past tense introductory verbs, the tense of the verb in the question must be changed:
>
> Can I help you? — *Eric asked if he could help Judy.*
>
> Do you want to go by air? — *He asked if she wanted to go by air.*
>
> Have you been to Rome before? — *He wanted to know if she had been to Rome before.*
>
> Will your friend meet you? — *He asked if her friend would meet her.*

2 Report Eric's questions.

EXAMPLE
Do you speak Italian? (Eric asked Judy)
Eric asked Judy if she spoke Italian.

1 Do you want to learn Italian? (Then he asked)
2 Do you know a good teacher? (He asked her)
3 Are you going to start soon? (He wanted to know)
4 Can I give you some lessons? (Eric wondered)
5 Have you heard of computer language lessons? (He asked)

3 Report the conversation. Choose Judy's replies from the box and write them in a paragraph with your answers from Exercise 2.

EXAMPLE
Eric asked Judy if she spoke Italian, *and she said she didn't speak any foreign languages.*

> , and she said she didn't speak any foreign languages.
>
> . Judy told him she hadn't tried to find one yet.
>
> , and Judy said she really ought to try.
>
> . She said she'd start when she found a teacher.
>
> , and she said she'd never heard anything about them.
>
> . Judy didn't know what to say, because she didn't think Eric would be a very good teacher!

4 Notice:

> When we report adverbs or adverbial phrases of time after a past tense introductory verb, we often have to change them.
>
> On Monday, Judy says, 'I'll buy my ticket tomorrow.' (**tomorrow** = Tuesday)
> On Tuesday, she says, 'I'm going to buy my ticket today.' (**today** = Tuesday)
> On Wednesday, she says, 'I bought my ticket yesterday.' (**yesterday** = Tuesday)
>
> Judy uses three different words for Tuesday, because her relation to Tuesday has changed.
> On Monday Judy said she'd buy her ticket *the next day/the day after.*
> On Tuesday she said she was going to buy her ticket *that day.*
> On Wednesday she said she'd bought it *the day before.*

5 Write direct questions/statements from these reported questions/statements.

EXAMPLE
Sally asked if Judy was going to the travel agency the next day.
Are you going to the travel agency tomorrow?

1 Judy said she'd gone to the travel agency the day before.
2 Sally asked if she was going to buy her ticket that day.
3 Judy said she was going to buy it the day after.
4 Then she told Sally that she was going to start her Italian lessons the next day.

6 Report what Eric asked Judy last week when she went to pay for her ticket.

EXAMPLE
Are you free this evening?
He asked me if I was free that evening.

1 Will you come to the cinema with me this evening?
2 Are you free this afternoon?
3 Do you want to see my computer this weekend?
4 Are you busy every evening this week?
5 Are you going to learn Italian this year?

Part D The short forms of **had** and **would**; writing practice

1 Notice:

> The short forms of **had** and **would** are the same: **'d** :
> *Eric asked Judy if she'd found an Italian teacher.* (**'d** = **had**)
> *Judy hoped she'd find a teacher soon.* (**'d** = **would**)
>
> The form of the word after **'d** usually tells us if **'d** = **had** or **would** : *had found, would find.*
> But with some verbs (e.g. **put, come**) the past participle is the same as the infinitive:
> *He said he'd put it on the table.*
> Adverbs/adverbial phrases can help us to decide if **'d** = **had** or **would**:
> *He said he'd put it on the table five minutes before.* (= **had**)
> *He said he'd put it on the table in five minutes.* (= **would**)

2 Show that you understand **'d** by adding *and she said she had/would.*

EXAMPLE
Eric asked Judy if she'd found an Italian teacher.
Eric asked Judy if she'd found an Italian teacher, and she said she had.

1 He asked her if she'd tried to find a teacher.
2 He asked if she'd have dinner with him.
3 He asked if she'd been to the Italian restaurant.
4 He asked if she'd ever used a computer.
5 He asked if she'd speak Italian to him.
6 He asked if she'd come and meet him after work that evening.

3 Complete the conversation:

A foreign tourist stops you in the street near your home, and asks you a lot of questions.

TOURIST: Excuse me, do you speak English?
STUDENT: *Yes/Yes, a little/Yes, I do/* . . .
TOURIST: Can you help me, please?
STUDENT: (Say that you'll try.)
TOURIST: Do you know the name of a good hotel?
STUDENT: (Suggest a hotel.)
TOURIST: Is it near here?
STUDENT: . . .
TOURIST: Which street is it in?
STUDENT: . . .
TOURIST: Can I walk there?
STUDENT: . . .
TOURIST: Is it better to take a bus or a taxi?
STUDENT: . . .
TOURIST: Thank you, you've been very helpful.
STUDENT: . . .

4 Report the conversation that you wrote for Exercise 3.

Begin: *One day last week someone stopped me in the street near my home. He/She was a (nationality) tourist. He/She asked if I* . . .
Use different verbs: **asked, wanted to know, said, told him/her, replied,** etc.
Finish: *Finally we shook hands and said goodbye.*

5 Imagine that you recently went to lunch with a friend. Describe what happened, using both direct speech and reported speech.

UNIT 13 Conditional clauses 2

Part A Read and answer

1 Read this passage:

Desert island

Mike and Bill have just seen 'Lord of the Flies'.
It's a film about some schoolboys on a desert
island.

MIKE: If I was on a desert island, I'd build a boat.
Then I'd be able to leave the island.
BILL: How would that help you? You'd probably
drown if you tried to leave the island. I
wouldn't try to build a boat.
MIKE: What would you do, then?
BILL: I'd look for some water. I'd try to find some
food. Then I'd wait.
MIKE: Wait? What for?
BILL: Oh, something would happen. Perhaps
someone would come.
MIKE: But what would you do all the time? It
would be boring.
BILL: I like doing nothing.
MIKE: If I did nothing, I'd be very bored. I'd want
to do something. I'd build a house first.
Then I'd think about my boat.
BILL: It would take weeks to build a house and a
boat.
MIKE: Well, that wouldn't matter. If we were on a
desert island, there would be plenty of time,
wouldn't there?
BILL: But how would you start?
MIKE: I don't know now. But if I had to, I'd find a
way of doing it.

2 Find the right words to complete the sentences.

EXAMPLE
I wouldn't __ to build a __.
I wouldn't try to build a boat.

1 I'd __ to find some __.
2 Something would __. Perhaps __ would __.
3 It would take __ to build a __ and a __.
4 If we were on a __ __, there would be __ of __.
5 But __ would you __?

3 Who do you think would do these things: Mike
or Bill?

EXAMPLE
__ would explore the whole island.
Mike would explore the whole island.

1 __ probably wouldn't want to explore the island.
2 __ would do most of the work.
3 __ wouldn't help very much.
4 __ would spend a lot of time sleeping.
5 __ would try to make some clothes.

4 Choose the right endings from the box for these
sentences.

EXAMPLE
If Mike was on a desert island, *he'd build a boat.*

1 If Mike was on a desert island, . . .
2 He'd probably drown if . . .
3 If Bill was on a desert island, . . .
4 He'd look for food and water, . . .
5 Mike would be bored . . .
6 Bill likes doing nothing, so he'd . . .

> he'd build a boat.
> be happy.
> he tried to leave the island.
> and then he'd wait.
> he wouldn't build a boat.
> if he didn't do anything.

Part B Using the conditional: **would** and **wouldn't (would not)**

1 Notice:

> In conversation and informal writing, use the
> short form of **would** (**'d**) after **I, you, he,
> she, we** and **they** :
> *I'd build a boat.*
> *Mike says he'd build a boat.*
> Use the full form **would** after **it** and at the
> end of a sentence:
> It **would** be difficult to build a boat.
> Bill wouldn't build a boat, but Mike says he
> **would**.
> Use the short form **wouldn't** except in
> formal writing or very emphatic sentences:
> *You'd like that, wouldn't you? No, I would
> not.*

2 What would *you* do on a desert island? Write
four sentences with **I'd** and four sentences with
I wouldn't. Choose items from the box.

EXAMPLES
I'd go swimming.
I wouldn't drink sea water.

go swimming	drink sea water
eat snakes	make some clothes
make a fire	eat strange fruit
climb trees	sleep in a tree
make a tent	sleep on the ground
look for water	try to catch fish

3 Write true sentences about yourself or people
you know.

EXAMPLE
Mike would build a boat, but __ wouldn't.
Mike would build a boat, but I/my grandmother/. . .
wouldn't.
(You decide.)

1 Bill wouldn't do any work, and __ wouldn't,
either.
2 He wouldn't work hard, but __ would.
3 Bill would lie in the sun and sleep, and __
would, too.
4 He'd be happy if he did nothing, but __
wouldn't.

4 Write questions.

Bill would wait.

EXAMPLE
Bill would wait. What for?
What would Bill wait for?

1 Mike would build a boat. Why?
2 He'd build something else first. What?
3 The boys would sleep somewhere. Where?
4 Bill would look for something. What?

5 Add question tags.

EXAMPLE
Life on a desert island would be difficult, . . .?
Life on a desert island would be difficult, wouldn't it?

1 Things wouldn't be easy, . . .?
2 People would get hungry, . . .?
3 Water would be the most important thing, . . .?
4 If you didn't have any water, you'd die, . . .?
5 But if it rained, there wouldn't be a problem,
. . .?
6 Then you wouldn't need to explore the island,
. . .?

6 Use your own ideas to complete this paragraph
about the things you would do on a desert
island.

If I was on a desert island, I'd . . . first, because
that would be the most important thing. Then I'd
. . . , and I'd probably . . . . If it was possible, I'd
. . . . If it was warm, I'd . . . , but of course if it
was cold, I wouldn't. I wouldn't do these things,
either: I wouldn't . . . or . . . ; and I certainly
wouldn't . . . , because that would be very
difficult/dangerous/stupid/. . . .

Part C Second conditional: unreal conditions about the present or the future

1 Notice:

> 'Unreal' conditions are conditions which are either not true or not probable:
> *If the boys were on a desert island, . . .* (we know this is untrue: they aren't on a desert island; they're coming out of the cinema.)
> *If you became president of your country tomorrow, . . .* (this is very improbable, but we can't say it isn't true, because it's about the future. We certainly do not expect that this will happen.)
>
> To express unreal conditions about the present or the future, we use the past tense in the **if** clause, and the conditional (**would/wouldn't** + verb) in the main clause:
> *If the boys were on a desert island, they'd do different things.*
> *Mike would probably drown if he tried to leave the island.*

2 Complete these conditions.

EXAMPLE
If I . . . , my teacher wouldn't be pleased.
If I lost my library book/failed my exams my teacher wouldn't be pleased.
(You decide.)

1 If I . . ., my friends would be very surprised.
2 If . . ., I'd be frightened.
3 If . . ., I'd probably be annoyed.
4 If . . ., I think that I'd be bored.

3 Write sentences about what you would do if you had to decide.

EXAMPLE
Imagine that you could live in Europe or America. Which would you choose?
If I could live in Europe or America, I'd choose Europe/America.
(You decide.)

1 Imagine you lived in London. Which would you buy: a house or a flat?
2 Imagine you won a lot of money. Would you stop working or keep your job?

3 Imagine you had to go from your country to England tomorrow. How would you go: by air or by sea or some other way?
4 Imagine someone offered you a good, but not very interesting, job. What would you say: yes or no?

4 Write sentences about what you would and wouldn't do if these very improbable things happened:

EXAMPLE
If an elephant came into my house, . . .
If an elephant came into my house, I'd run away/scream/. . . .
(You decide.)

1 If I saw a tiger in my sitting room, . . .
2 If someone said I could go to the moon next year, . . .
3 If I became president/prime minister of (country) tomorrow, . . .
4 If I was told that the world was really flat, . . .

5 Put these sentences into the correct order and write them in a paragraph. Sentence *a* is the first sentence.

a Bill doesn't work very hard at school.
b If he passed his exams, he'd go into the next class.
c That's why he doesn't work very hard!
d If he worked harder, he'd pass his exams.
e If he went into the next class, he'd have to work even harder.

6 Write a similar paragraph from these notes.

Anne: always late for work; if not late, better job; if better, more interesting; if more interesting, like it more; but doesn't like it, that's why always late.

Part D Word study; writing practice

1 Notice:

Mike says he would be *bored* if he did
nothing. He thinks it would be *boring*.
Other pairs of adjectives like this are:
interesting   interested (in something)
annoying   annoyed
surprising   surprised
tiring   tired (of something)
The adjectives which end with **-ing** can
describe people and things, and can go in
front of nouns, or after the verb **to be**:
an interesting person, that's interesting.
The adjectives which end with **-ed** usually
describe people, and do not often go in front
of nouns:
Bill wouldn't be interested in building a boat.

2 Complete the sentences with the right words.

EXAMPLE
You'd get ___ of fish if you ate it every day. (tiring,
tired)
You'd get tired of fish if you ate it every day.

1 Mike has always been ___ in making things.
   (interesting, interested)
2 If Bill helped Mike with the boat, Mike would
   be ___. (surprising, surprised)
3 Bill would probably say that hard work was ___.
   (tiring, tired)
4 That would be a very ___ thing to say. (annoying,
   annoyed)

3 Prepare for writing by answering questions
about these three difficult situations. Make
short notes.

Alone in the jungle after a plane crash.

Lost in a snow storm in the mountains.

Without any petrol in the middle of the desert.

1 Where would these things be a problem: animals
   and/or insects? thirst? hunger? heat? cold?
2 What would you do about these problems?
3 Would you stay in each place, or would you try
   to leave?
4 What wouldn't you do in each situation?

4 Choose one of the three situations, and write a
conversation between yourself and someone
who has different ideas. Before you start, look
back at Part A Exercise 1, but use your own
ideas, of course. Building a boat probably
wouldn't be useful in these situations!

Begin: *If you were alone in the jungle after your
plane had crashed, what would you do?*
OR *If you were lost in a snowstorm in the mountains,
what would you do?*
OR *If you were in the middle of the desert and you
didn't have any petrol, what would you do?*

UNIT 14 Reported and indirect commands, requests and advice

Part A Read and answer

1 Read this passage:

Sheila's first day

Today is Sheila's first day in a new job. She has just arrived.

ALAN: Hello, are you the new assistant?

SHEILA: Yes, I'm Sheila Fraser. How do you do?

ALAN: My name's Alan Lees. My office is next to yours. Come upstairs and I'll show you everything.

SHEILA: Thank you. Where can I leave my coat?

ALAN: Take it with you. There's a cloakroom upstairs. Don't leave it here.

(They go upstairs.)

ALAN: Here's your office. You should keep it tidy, or Miss Frost will complain. This is your desk. Don't leave a lot of papers on it. Miss Frost doesn't like untidy people.

SHEILA: Excuse me, who's Miss Frost?

ALAN: She's your boss. Listen. In the morning, don't say 'Hello' to her. Say 'Good morning, Miss Frost.' And call me Mr Lees when you're talking about me. Don't call me Alan.

SHEILA: I hope I'll remember.

ALAN: Oh, don't worry. There's another assistant. Her name's Barbara. Ask her if you have any problems. That's my advice.

2 Find the right words to complete the sentences:

EXAMPLE
Alan told Sheila to come ___ and said he'd ___ her everything.
Alan told Sheila to come upstairs and said he'd show her everything.

1 He told her to take her ___ with her.
2 He advised her to keep her ___ tidy.
3 He told her not to leave a lot of ___ on her ___.
4 He told her not to say ___ to ___ ___.
5 Then he told Sheila to call him ___ ___ when she was ___ about him.

3 Complete these sentences with **to** or **not to**:

EXAMPLE
Alan told Sheila ___ leave her coat downstairs.
Alan told Sheila not to leave her coat downstairs.

1 He advised Sheila ___ keep her office tidy.
2 He told her ___ say good morning to Miss Frost.
3 He told her ___ call him Alan when she was talking about him.
4 Finally he told her ___ worry.

4 Choose the right sentences from the box to describe Sheila's questions.

EXAMPLE
Excuse me, where's the cafeteria, please?
She's asking someone to show her the way.

1 Excuse me, where's the cafeteria, please?
2 Excuse me, Miss Frost, is this the right address?
3 I don't understand this, Alan. Do you?
4 Could you help me with the computer, please?

She's asking	someone Alan Miss Frost	to	show her the way. explain something. help her with a machine. check an address.

Part B Reporting commands

1 Notice:

> Imperatives and negative imperatives are
> used in direct commands:
> *Come upstairs. Don't worry.*
> We report commands with **tell** :
> **tell** + someone + (**not**) **to** + infinitive + . . .
> *Alan told Sheila   to   come upstairs.*
> *He told her   not to   worry.*

2 Report these commands.
   Begin: *Barbara told Sheila*

EXAMPLE
Go and see Miss Frost every morning.
Barbara told Sheila to go and see Miss Frost every morning.

1 Type her letters first.
2 Don't leave them until after lunch.
3 Check all the addresses.
4 Don't ask Miss Frost too many questions.
5 Lock your office at night.
6 Don't leave the window open.

3 Notice:

> Reported commands do not show person or
> tense, but other verbs in the sentence must
> be changed after a past tense introductory verb:
> Ask me if you need help.
> *Barbara told Sheila to ask her if she needed help.*

4 Report these sentences:

EXAMPLE
Lock the door when you leave. (Barbara told Sheila)
Barbara told Sheila to lock the door when she left.

1 Open the window when you arrive in the morning. (Barbara told her)
2 Ask me if you have a problem. (She told Sheila)
3 Turn the computer off when you've finished with it. (Alan told her)

4 Answer these letters at once if you can. (Miss Frost told Sheila)
5 But don't worry if you can't start at once. (But then she told her)

5 Notice:

> We use **order** someone (not) to do
> something when we report very strong
> commands or orders which must be obeyed:
> Stop!   *The policeman ordered*
>   *the man to stop.*
> Return in one hour. *The officer ordered the*
>   *soldiers to return in one hour.*
>
> Notice that we can also report these strong
> orders with **tell,** but we cannot use **order** to
> report Alan's or Barbara's words. Use **order**
> only when there is a very good reason.

6 Complete these sentences with **told** or **ordered**.

EXAMPLE
The general ___ the officers to meet him in his room.
The general ordered the officers to meet him in his room.

1 Alan ___ Sheila to be very polite to Miss Frost.
2 Sheila's mother ___ her not to wear trousers on her first day.
3 The robbers ___ everyone in the bank to lie on the floor.
4 Then they ___ the manager to give them all the money in the bank.

7 Who said these sentences? Who did they say them to? You decide, and report the sentences with **told**.

EXAMPLE
Come in.
Miss Frost told Sheila to come in.
OR *The doctor told the next patient to come in.*

| 1 Come in | 2 Be careful | 3 Don't shout. |
| 4 Turn the TV off. | 5 Send me a postcard. | 6 Don't forget your tickets. |

Part C Reporting requests and advice

1 Notice:

> Imperatives are also used to ask people to do things, i.e. to make requests:
> *Give me the newspaper, please.*
> *Please don't finish the cakes.*
> We report requests with **ask**:
>
> | | **ask** + someone + (**not**) **to** + infinitive + . . . | | | |
> |---|---|---|---|---|
> | *I* | *asked* | *my sister* | *to* | *give me the newspaper.* |
> | *Mother* | *asked* | *us* | *not to* | *finish the cakes.* |
>
> Notice that requests can also have other forms:
> *Can/could/will/would you help me (please)?*
> It is shorter and easier to report:
> *The old lady asked the policeman to help her.*
> than to use an indirect question:
> *The old lady asked the policeman if he could/would help her.*

2 Complete these requests:

EXAMPLE
The old lady asked the policeman to . . .
The old lady asked the policeman to tell her the time/stop the traffic/ . . .
(You decide.)

1 Sheila asked Barbara to . . .
2 The students asked their teacher not to . . .
3 The teacher asked one of the girls to . . .
4 The little girl asked the policeman to . . .
5 The conductor of the orchestra asked the people at the concert not to . . .

3 Notice:

> We can give advice with imperatives and with other forms:
> *Ask Barbara. That's my advice.*
> *You shouldn't listen to Alan.*
>
> We report advice with **advise**:
>
> | | **advise** + someone + (**not**) **to** + infinitive + . . . | | | |
> |---|---|---|---|---|
> | *Alan* | *advised* | *Sheila* | *to* | *ask* | *Barbara.* |
> | *Barbara* | *advised* | *her* | *not to* | *listen* | *to Alan.* |

4 Report the advice that Sheila was given, with **advised her**.

EXAMPLE
BARBARA: Don't worry about Miss Frost.
Barbara advised her not to worry about Miss Frost.

1 BARBARA: This is my advice: check your spelling.
2 BARBARA: You should use a dictionary.
3 MISS FROST: Don't believe all that Alan says.
4 MISS FROST: Ask Barbara if you need help.

5 Read this conversation, and then choose the right sentences from the box to report it:

EXAMPLE
ALAN: Sell that old car, Dad.
Alan told his father to sell his car.

1 ALAN: Sell that old car, Dad.
2 MR LEES: Well, can you think of a price?
3 ALAN: If it was mine, I'd sell it for £150. Yes, that's my advice: ask for £150, not more.
4 MR LEES: Would you help me to write an advertisement?
5 ALAN: Of course. Why don't you begin by saying that it's in very good condition?
6 MR LEES: But it isn't. Don't talk nonsense. It's twenty years old.

Alan Mr Lees	told asked advised	his father Alan	to not to

sell his car.
ask for more than £150.
help him with an advertisement.
suggest a price.
talk nonsense.
say the car was in good condition.

Part D Punctuation in reported speech; review; writing practice

1 Notice:

> 1 There is a comma after **said, asked, told me** etc in direct speech:
> *The manager said, 'Come in.' Then he asked, 'What do you want?'*
>
> 2 There is never a comma between an introductory verb and a reported sentence:
> *The manager told me to come in and asked what I wanted.*
>
> 3 The form of the introductory verb decides the punctuation at the end of a reported sentence:
> *She told me to come in. (She told* is a statement.)
> *Did she ask you to help her? (Did she ask* is a question.)

2 Rewrite these sentences with the correct punctuation. Sheila is describing her first day:

WHEN I SAW MY NEW BOSS I SAID GOOD MORNING MISS FROST SHE SAID HELLO YOURE SHEILA ARENT YOU THEN SHE TOLD ME TO GO TO HER IF I WANTED TO KNOW ANYTHING I DIDNT THINK SHED BE SO FRIENDLY

THEN SHE TOLD ME NOT TO LISTEN TO ALAN SHE SAID HE ALWAYS TELLS NEW PEOPLE SILLY STORIES ABOUT ME

ALAN LAUGHED WHEN I TOLD HIM THAT AND SAID EVERYONE CALLED HER FROSTY NOW I REALLY DONT KNOW WHETHER HES TELLING THE TRUTH OR NOT

4 Choose the right words to describe what Sheila thought Miss Frost would be like.

After Alan had talked to Sheila, she $\left\{ \begin{array}{l} \text{thought} \\ \text{didn't think} \end{array} \right\}$ she was going to like Miss Frost very much. She

expected that Miss Frost would be $\left\{ \begin{array}{l} \text{friendly.} \\ \text{unfriendly.} \end{array} \right\}$

Sheila thought she would probably be $\left\{ \begin{array}{l} \text{quite young,} \\ \text{about fifty,} \end{array} \right\}$

and that working for her would be $\left\{ \begin{array}{l} \text{easy.} \\ \text{difficult.} \end{array} \right\}$

5 Write a paragraph about what Sheila thought after she'd met Miss Frost.

Begin: *But when Sheila had met Miss Frost, she thought she was going to enjoy her new job.*

6 Complete the conversation between Sheila and Alan two weeks later.

SHEILA: Why did you tell me all these things about Miss Frost?

ALAN: What things? I only told you to ... I didn't say ...

3 Review of introductory verbs in indirect and reported speech.

Statements	**say**(to someone)/**tell**(someone)/**know/think** /(that); **reply/answer that**
Questions	**ask** (someone)/**know/wonder** + **if**/question word
Commands etc	**tell/order/ask/advise** someone + (**not**) **to** + infinitive

EXAMPLES:
Sheila said (that) she'd enjoyed her first day.
Her mother asked (her) if the office was busy, and Sheila replied that it was very busy.
Sheila doesn't know if she can believe Alan.
She wonders why he told her those stories about Miss Frost.
First he told her (that) she must be very polite to Miss Frost.
Then Miss Frost told Sheila not to listen to Alan.
Sheila asked Barbara to explain.
But Barbara only said (that) she didn't know why Alan had said that.

Index

Answer key

Unit 1

Part A Exercise 2: 1 She looked cleverer.
2 Her hair was curlier than that, too. 3 Yes,
she had a longer nose than that. 4 I think
she looked more intelligent than this woman.
5 Her face was rounder than that. 6 She had
shorter hair. 7 It was thinner, too. 8 Her
mouth was much wider.

Exercise 3: 2 rounder 3 longer, thinner
4 bigger, wider 5 cleverer, more intelligent

Exercise 4: Joan saw C.

Part B Exercise 2: 1 . . . is nicer than . . .
2 . . . are friendlier than . . . 3 . . . is hotter
than . . . 4 . . . are easier than . . . 5 . . .
are cheaper than . . . 6 . . . are safer than . . .

Exercise 4: 1 hot, hottest 2 big, bigger
3 largest, larger 4 busy, busier

Exercise 6: 1 better 2 bad, worst 3 better,
good 4 worse 5 best, worst

Part C Exercise 5: 1 difficult, more difficult
2 most exciting, most exciting 3 more
expensive, the most expensive, more
expensive

Part D Exercise 2: 1 angrier, angriest
2 more/most annoyed 3 earlier, earliest
4 healthier, healthiest 5 more/most helpful
6 more/most exciting 7 more/most
marvellous 8 shallower, shallowest
9 simpler, simplest 10 stranger, strangest
11 more/most tiring 12 more/most useless

Exercise 3: 1 a 2 b 3 b 4 a 5 a

Unit 2

Part A Exercise 2: 1 Liverham 2 Liverham
3 Tottenpool, Liverham 4 Liverham
5 Tottenpool 6 Liverham 7 Liverham

Exercise 3: 1 But our players were so good
that Liverham never got another chance.
2 We weren't fast enough to score a goal,
that's all. 3 They played too slowly.
4 They didn't work hard enough. 5 They
were so fast that Liverham never got the ball.
6 We all hope that Liverham will play well
enough to win their big match in Spain next
week. 7 Liverham didn't play well enough
to win.

Exercise 4: 1 Our team played well enough
to win the World Cup! 2 They were so fast
that Liverham never got the ball. 3 We
weren't fast enough to score a goal, that's all.
4 But our players were so good that Liverham
never got another chance. 5 We all hope that
Liverham will play well enough to win their big
match in Spain next week.

Part B Exercise 2: low . . . high; narrow
. . . wide; old . . . new; shallow . . . deep;
short . . . long; slow . . . quick; young . . .
old

Exercise 3: 1 is too shallow. It isn't deep
enough. 2 's/is too young. He isn't old
enough. 3 were too slow. They weren't
quick enough. 4 's/is too old. It isn't new
enough. 5 're/are too short. They aren't long
enough. 6 is too narrow. It isn't wide
enough. 7 is too low. It isn't high enough.

Exercise 5: 1 Tottenpool played well enough
to win the cup. 2 The other team didn't
work hard enough to get a goal. 3 They were
too tired to work hard. 4 They had been too
busy to practise. 5 We hope they'll play well
enough to win next week.

Part C Exercise 2: 1 It's so wet that you'll
need an umbrella. 2 That dress is so
expensive that Joan can't afford it. 3 The
film was so boring that we came home 4 I
worked so hard that I got very hungry.
5 The boy answered so quietly that the
teacher couldn't hear him. 6 Mrs Brown's
suitcase was so heavy that she couldn't carry
it. 7 It was so late when they arrived that
they had to take a taxi.

Exercise 3: 1 noisily 2 angry 3 loudly
4 quiet 5 quietly

Part D Exercise 2: 1 slowly . . . late 2 slow
. . . slow 3 dangerous . . . safely 4 good
. . . slow . . . badly

Unit 3

Part A Exercise 2: 1 Two main roads near
Glasgow are blocked by trees. 2 High tides
are expected again tonight. 3 Four people
were rescued by helicopter this afternoon.
4 More storms are expected tomorrow.

Exercise 3: 1 are reported in the south.
2 have been flooded near Dover. 3 was
blown over by the wind. 4 have been lost.
5 was found two miles inland.

Exercise 4: 2 are closed in Scotland.
3 heavy rain is reported. 4 have flooded
parts of the east coast. 5 have been flooded
in the west. 6 are expected tomorrow.

Part B Exercise 2: 1 He was examined.
2 His wife was told about the accident.
3 She was brought to the hospital. 4 The
lorry-driver was allowed to go home. 5 He
was advised to go to bed and rest. 6 A taxi
was ordered. 7 The man and his wife were
taken home.

Exercise 3: 1 The accident was caused by
high winds. 2 Two main roads were blocked
by trees. 3 Many roads were closed by the
police. 4 Many areas were flooded by sea
water. 5 A small boat was found in a field
by two children. 6 Two villages were flooded
by a river. 7 A helicopter was used by the
police.

Exercise 4: 1 Meals aren't prepared by a
waiter. They're prepared by a cook.
2–5 *students' own answers* 6 Aeroplanes aren't
usually flown by women. They're usually
flown by men.

Exercise 5: 1 flooded 2 were covered 3 was
interviewed 4 told 5 found 6 were found
7 flooded 8 interviewed

Part C Exercise 2: 1 These roads have been
closed by the police. 2 The roads will
not/won't be opened until the trees have been
moved. 3 Many small boats have been lost
in the east. 4 Many farms have been flooded
by sea water. 5 Helicopters have been used
in Wales. 6 The army has been asked to
help. 7 Some soldiers will be sent to Wales
tonight.

Exercise 3: 1 been seen 2 said 3 was lost
4 be sent 5 take 6 be taken 7 found 8 be
compared 9 be found 10 found

Exercise 4: 1 The *Isabella* was lost about
1585. 2 The ship will be explored by divers.
3 Special cameras will be needed to take
photographs. 4 A picture of the *Isabella* has
been found in a museum. 5 Perhaps (some)
gold will be found on the *Isabella*. 6 Gold
has already been found in other Spanish
ships.

Exercise 5: 1 a 2 b 3 a 4 a 5 a

Part D Exercise 2: 1 Child found 2 Jobs
planned 3 Jewels stolen

Exercise 3: 1 *six* 2 *the first paragraph*
3 *four* 4 *It's about the forecast for tomorrow.*

Unit 4

Part A Exercise 2: 1 I've come to help her.
2 But she doesn't speak it very well. 3 I'll
tell you what she says. 4 I'll give your
mother something for her headaches, and
some sleeping pills. 5 But I want to see her
again. 6 You must bring her back next
week.

Exercise 3: 1 She gets them almost every day.
2 She never sleeps well. 3 She doesn't go to
sleep easily. 4 She often wakes up during the
night.

Exercise 4: 1 understood English, . . . speak
it very well. 2 very bad headaches. 3 slept
well. 4 woke up during the night.
5 something for her headaches and some
sleeping pills. 6 to see her again. 7 back
next week.

Part B Exercise 2: 1 she feels much better.
2 he wants to examine her eyes. 3 she must
go to the eye hospital. 4 she doesn't want to
go to the hospital. 5 he'll/he will phone the
hospital now.

Exercise 3: 1 The eye doctor/He tells Mrs
Patel/her that it's a very small operation.
2 Mary tells her mother that it will help her
eyes. 3 Mrs Patel tells Mary/her that she
doesn't want to have an operation. 4 Mary
tells Mrs Patel/her mother/her that she'll feel
much better afterwards. 5 Mrs Patel tells the
doctor that her headaches have stopped.
6 The doctor/He tells Mrs Patel/her that she
needs this operation. 7 Mary tells Mrs
Patel/her mother/her that she can't take pills
all her life. 8 Mrs Patel tells Mary that she
doesn't want to go into hospital. 9 The
doctor tells Mary that she must try to
persuade her mother.

Exercise 4: 2 is afraid of hospitals. 3 won't
agree. 4 have got better. 5 she doesn't need
the operation. 6 will explain to her mother.
7 have the operation. 8. Mrs Patel will refuse.

Part C Exercise 2: He said . . . 1 she
needed an operation. 2 it was very simple.
3 it wouldn't be painful. 4 her headaches
would stop. 5 he knew Mrs Patel was afraid.
6 the operation was really necessary.

Exercise 3: 1 Mrs Patel told Mary that she
didn't want to have an operation. 2 Mrs
Patel told the doctor that her headaches had
stopped. 3 Mary told her mother that the

pills had helped her headaches. 4 The doctor told Mrs Patel that her eyes would be much better after the operation. 5 The doctor told Mary that Mrs Patel/her mother really needed the operation.

Exercise 5: 1 Mary said she knew she must persuade her mother. 2 Mrs Patel said she couldn't take time off work. 3 Mary said Mrs Patel/her mother must tell her boss about the operation. 4 The doctor said he could write to her mother's/Mrs Patel's boss. 5 Mrs Patel said perhaps she could ask for a holiday. 6 Mary said she/Mrs Patel mustn't do that.

Part D Exercise 2: I told you 1 it was difficult. 2 Mary had arrived. 3 she was a librarian. 4 she'd/had gone to London. 5 it was impossible. 6 she was looking for a new job. 7 she'd/had found a new job. 8 it was a good job.

Exercise 3: 1 a,c,b 2 b,c,a 3 a,c,d,b,e

Exercise 4: 1 needed 2 was 3 wasn't 4 couldn't 5 can't 6 isn't 7 would 8 understands 9 'll

Unit 5

Part A Exercise 2: 1 The police doctor said the man had died about eight hours before. 2 Therefore the murder had probably happened between midnight and one o'clock. 3 The first man said he had been at home the whole evening. 4 They had been to the cinema together. 5 He had got home about eleven o'clock.

Exercise 3: 1 first man . . . gone to bed 2 second man . . . the evening . . . some friends. 3 third man . . . a knife 4 asleep . . . midnight 5 Jim Wilson

Exercise 4: but someone knew. . . 2 it had happened at midnight. 3 it was Jim Wilson. 4 that a knife had been used.

Part B Exercise 2: He said . . . 1 he'd/he had never known him well. 2 he'd/he had never telephoned him. 3 he hadn't worked with Wilson. 4 he hadn't met his wife. 5 they'd/they had never talked about business. 6 Wilson had never borrowed any money from him.

Exercise 4: She told the police that . . . 1 her husband hadn't been worried. 2 he hadn't told her the name of the person. 3 he'd/he had left the house at 11.15. 4 he'd/he had taken a lot of money with him. 5 he'd/he had told her to go to bed. 6 the same thing had happened in September.

Exercise 6: 1 I went to bed at 10.30. 2 I've never met Jim Wilson. 3 I met my friends after dinner. 4 We left the cinema at 10.15. 5 I've never owned a knife. 6 I didn't leave my house after dinner.

Exercise 7: 2 to come and meet him. 3 had met each other at 11.30. 4 about some business first. 5 had started. 6 and killed Wilson. 7 because he had been afraid.

Part C Exercise 2: 1 It had started to rain. 2 Everyone had gone home. 3 The football match had finished. 4 The players had left.

Exercise 3: He had never . . . 1 seen an oil well before. 2 met a cowboy before. 3 visited a cattle ranch before. 4 ridden a horse before. 5 talked to a millionaire before.

Exercise 4: 1 It was the largest steak he had ever eaten. 2 It was the most expensive shop he had ever seen. 3 They were the richest people he had ever met. 4 They were the best photographs he had ever taken. 5 They were the most fantastic stories he had ever heard.

Exercise 6: 1 I had already finished my book. 2 Mary had already seen that film. 3 Peter had already gone out. 4 Mrs Patel had already bought some fruit.

Part D Exercise 2: 1 They made a cup of tea and went to bed. 2 The second man went out and met some friends. 3 He said they'd gone to the cinema and seen a film. 4 After the film he'd said goodbye and come home. 5 The third man finally told the police that Wilson had borrowed some money and hadn't paid it back. 6 He said he had phoned Wilson and asked for the money. 7 Wilson had promised to meet him and bring the money.

Unit 6

Part A Exercise 2: 1 They shouldn't forget that jobs are very difficult to find. 2 These people ought to remember that many young people don't have jobs. 3 Other people ought not to decide things for us.

Exercise 3: 1 to pass his exams 2 Should . . . go back 3 remember . . . young people . . . jobs 4 forget . . . jobs . . . very difficult

Exercise 5: 2 They ought to be paid less. 3 They should let us decide. 4 What should I do.

Part B Exercise 2: 1 should 2 should 3 ought 4 should 5 shouldn't 6 ought

Exercise 4: 1 He ought to do his homework. 2 He ought to be polite to his teachers. 3 He ought not to borrow Ben's radio without asking. 4 He ought to put the radio back. 5 He ought not to hide Ben's shoes. 6 He ought to say 'please' and 'thank you'. 7 He ought not to read Ben's letters. 8 He ought to obey his mother.

Exercise 6: 1 he ought not to say things like that. 2 she should really get angry with Sam. 3 he should find a job. 4 Ben said he ought to keep quiet. 5 Sam he should get ready for school.

Part C Exercise 3: Shouldn't you . . . 1 cover the table? 2 use a bigger brush? 3 move the ladder? 4 be more careful? 5 say you're sorry? 6 clean the floor?

Part D Exercise 2: 1 unemployment (noun) 2 argue (verb) 3 difficult (adjective) 4 life (noun) 5 information (noun) 6 advice (noun) 7 painter (noun)

Exercise 4: I don't think . . . 1 Ben should be so careless. 2 Mr Jackson should shout. 3 he should show that he dislikes young people. 4 he should say that everything is wrong.

Unit 7

Part A Exercise 2: 1 which didn't have any doors or windows. 2 who owned the house 3 that was in his 4 that had been in the house

Exercise 3: 1 It belonged to the girl who was with him. 2 Things that are difficult to understand often happen in dreams. 3 The only thing that was in the room was an old bicycle. 4 Then the man who owned the house arrived.

Exercise 4: 2 which was for sale. 3 that didn't belong to him. 4 was with him. 5 that didn't have any doors! 6 that was in the room. 7 and Tim bought the house from him. 8 which was only a pile of stones.

Part B Exercise 2: 1 which 2 who 3 which 4 which 5 who 6 who

Exercise 4: 1 The books are on the table which is near the door. 2 The books that are from the library are on the table. 3 You should keep meat which has been cooked in a refrigerator. 4 Children often enjoy TV programmes that are about animals. 5 Children who like animals often want to have a pet. 6 The teacher congratulated the students who had passed the exam. 7 The people who were at the bus stop were glad to see the bus.

Exercise 5: 1 Tim was in a car which didn't belong to him. 2 He was with the girl who owned the car. 3 Tim bought the house from the man who wanted to sell it. 4 The house which was for sale was very strange. 5 The man who sold the house had gone. 6 Tim found the bicycle which had been in the empty room.

Exercise 6: 1 who worked in Tim's office. 2 which had been for sale. 3 who had gone there with him. 4 that led to the house.

Part C Exercise 2: 1 That man's house is for sale. 2 That girl's mother is Russian. 3 That women's house is next to the hospital. 4 That man's daughter is in the Olympic team.

Exercise 3: That's the . . . 1 woman whose husband works in China. 2 girl whose dress cost £200. 3 man whose wife is an actress. 4 boy whose father comes from Yugoslavia.

Exercise 4: 1 who 2 whose 3 whose 4 who 5 whose 6 who 7 who

Exercise 5: Example and 6, 1 and 5, 2 and 4, 3 and 7

Part D Exercise 2: 1 whose 2 who's 3 whose 4 who's 5 who's 6 whose

Unit 8

Part A Exercise 2: 1 car . . . girl . . . with 2 man . . . arrived 3 bicycle . . . seen . . . house 4 strangest . . . ever

Exercise 3: 1 We were in a room that didn't have any doors or windows. 2 I gave him all the money I had and he left. 3 Then I saw that the house I had bought was only a pile of stones. 4 I had spent all my money on a house that was worth nothing. 5 You're going to spend a lot of money on something that is completely useless.

Part B Exercise 2: 1 They'd borrowed the suitcases. 2 They'd borrowed the car. 3 He liked the girl. 4 He liked the record. 5 She had received the letters. 6 She had received the parcel.

Exercise 3: 1 The man told Tim about a house that he wanted to sell. 2 The bicycle that they saw was very old. 3 Tim gave the man the money that he had in his pocket.

4 He bought a house that he didn't really want. 5 Madam Zaza was the name of the fortune teller that Tim asked about his dream. 6 She gave him an explanation that he didn't like.

Exercise 5: 1 that he was in 2 that he paid for 3 that he bought it from 4 that Madam Zaza gets money from

Part C Exercise 2: 1 The book that I'm reading is about aeroplanes. 2 Why didn't you eat the cake that I made for you? 3 Go and pay for the things that you've chosen. 4 The cat's eating something that it found in the garden.

Exercise 3: It was . . . 1 the most exciting film she had ever seen. 2 the most interesting TV programme they had ever watched. 3 the longest letter she had ever written. 4 the cleverest explanation she had ever thought of.

Exercise 5: 1 b 2 a 3 b 4 a

Exercise 6: *Contact clauses are possible after clothes, things, explanation*

Exercise 7: *Questions with contact clauses on lines 1, 6 and 16. Statements with contact clauses on lines 18, 19 and 27.*

Unit 9

Part A Exercise 1: 1 Dial . . . fire 2 police . . . ambulance 3 999 4 emergency . . . calls

Exercise 2: 1 freezes 2 steam 3 water 4 ice 5 heated

Exercise 3: 2 he'll be all right. 3 if he has some letters for that house. 4 he won't have to go in. 5 if he doesn't have to go in

Exercise 4: 1 gets . . . won't 2 she'll . . . stop 3 send . . . stops 4 She's . . . does

Part B Exercise 2: 1 If steam meets something cold, it changes into water. 2 If children are happy, they usually behave well. 3 If people work hard, they are often successful. 4 If animals are looked after well, they are usually healthy.

Exercise 4: 1 If she sees him, she tells him to stop. 2 If she gets really angry, she sends him to bed. 3 If Tom promises to be good, she says he can get up. 4 If Tom is very naughty, his mother tells his father.

Part C Exercise 2: 1 bites . . . won't take 2 want . . . will have 3 will go . . . isn't 4 go . . . 'll/will 5 will catch . . . don't run away 6 catches . . . won't do

Exercise 5: 1 You'll forget it if you don't write it down. 2 We'll miss the bus if you/we don't hurry. 3 I'll go away if you don't stop it. 4 You'll drop it if you aren't careful. 5 You'll be hungry later if you don't have a sandwich now. 6 You'll be very tired tomorrow if you don't go to bed. 7 We'll be late if you don't drive faster. 8 I'll never finish my homework if you don't tell me the answer.

Part D Exercise 2: 1 can . . . can't 2 don't . . . do 3 do . . . don't 4 does . . . doesn't 5 do . . . don't

Unit 10

Part A Exercise 2: 1 were . . . were making . . . elephants 2 arrived . . . three young elephants 3 playing 4 was working . . . heard . . . zoo . . . England 5 seemed . . . saw 6 was playing . . . usual

Exercise 3: 2 was acting in the film. 3 were acting in it too. 4 were playing together in a river. 5 was teaching them to act. 6 was throwing water at the others.

Exercise 4: 1 saw 2 playing 3 look 4 enjoying 5 unhappy

Part B Exercise 2: 1 was acting 2 was playing 3 were standing 4 were watching 5 weren't looking 6 was listening

Exercise 4: 1 was having 2 was 3 had 4 were 5 was 6 was having 7 was

Part C Exercise 2: 1 was working . . . heard 2 visited . . . was playing 3 wasn't doing . . . went 4 was standing . . . arrived 5 was sitting . . . heard

Exercise 4: while . . . 2 they were discussing Hekima. 3 she was making some coffee. 4 he was washing the dishes. 5 she was drinking her coffee. 6 she was/they were watching the programme.

Exercise 5: 2 that Hekima had died. 3 while I was watching television. 4 answered the telephone. 5 I knew that he had some bad news. 6 he said sadly.

Part D Exercise 2: 1 handbag. 2 it!' 3 Hekima: 'Elephants' and 'Jungle Story'. 4 lions! 5 Hekima: her friendliness and her intelligence. 6 problems: she became wild and dangerous, and she attacked people. 7 friend. Poor Carol!

Unit 11

Part A Exercise 2: 1 asks 2 doesn't ask 3 doesn't ask 4 asks 5 asks 6 doesn't ask

Exercise 3: 1 interested . . . things 2 advertisement 3 Jack Baker 4 Ron . . . Liz 5 Jack/Jack Baker/Mr Baker . . . work

Exercise 4: 1 Did you see an advertisement? 2 Well, why do you want this job? 3 Was it Jack Baker? 4 What did he say about his work?

Exercise 5: 1 Soon? 2 Until next month? 3 In London? 4 The centre? 5 Does she have a good job?

Part B Exercise 2: 2 where they're/they are going. 3 How much does Ron earn? 4 why she loves him. 5 How long has Jack worked there? 6 how Jack likes his job.

Exercise 4: Liz asks Ron . . . 1 how many hours he works every week. 2 what his salary is. 3 how long he has had his present job. 4 where his wife works. 5 which parts of the country he knows. 6 when he can start working for them.

Exercise 6: 1 Who spoke to you? 2 Who did you meet? 3 Who was most helpful? 4 Who will you work with?

Part C Exercise 2: 1 Why are you looking for a new job? 2 How did you hear about the job? 3 When can you start? 4 How will your wife feel about moving to another city?

Exercise 3: She asked him . . . 1 what he would say to his boss. 2 how much they were going to pay him. 3 where they would have to live. 4 how she was going to find a new job. 5 what a new house would cost.

Exercise 4: 1 how many 2 how much 3 what time 4 how old 5 how long

Part D Exercise 2: 1 Did someone say . . . Odeon? 2 No one told me . . . was. 3 I don't know . . . is. 4 she didn't say . . . going. 5 did she tell you . . . back? 6 I wonder . . . starts.

Exercise 3: *introductory phrase* + who discovered America./where Timbuktu is./when the first moon landing was./what the capital of Finland is./how long a football match lasts./which language has the most speakers. ANSWERS: Columbus, Mali, 1969, Helsinki, 90 minutes, Chinese has the most native speakers, but if non-native speakers are included, then English has the most.

Unit 12

Part A Exercise 2: 1 air fare . . . expensive 2 wants . . . week . . . month 3 stay . . . month 4 going . . . ticket 5 cheapest 6 cheaper . . . train

Exercise 3: 1 asks 2 asks 3 doesn't ask 4 asks 5 asks 6 doesn't ask

Exercise 4: 1 by train. 2 the train fare was. 3 train journey took. 4 change trains. 5 to book a seat now.

Part B Exercise 2: 2 if she will go by train. 3 Can she afford £172? 4 if she likes flying. 5 Is she going to stay in a hotel? 6 if she knows anyone in Rome. 7 Is she going alone?

Exercise 3: Do you know . . . 1 if Judy speaks any foreign languages? 2 if she's/she has been to Italy before? 3 if she can stay with her friends in Rome? 4 if she is going with her sister? 5 if Judy and her sister like Italian food? 6 if Judy will have to get a new passport?

Exercise 5: Eric asks Judy whether . . . 1 she'll/she will stay less than a month or more than a month. 2 she wants to leave on the fourth or the fifth. 3 she's/she is going to travel first class or not. 4 she wants to pay today or when she gets the ticket. 5 she's/she is going to pay by cheque or in cash.

Part C Exercise 2: 1 Then he asked if she wanted to learn Italian. 2 He asked her if she knew a good teacher. 3 He wanted to know if she was going to start soon. 4 Eric wondered if he could give her some lessons. 5 He asked if she'd/she had heard of computer language lessons.

Exercise 3: (*numbers refer to items in Exercise 2 above*) 1 and Judy said she really ought to try. 2 Judy told him she hadn't tried to find one yet. 3 She said she'd start when she found a teacher. 4 Judy didn't know what to say because she didn't think Eric would be a very good teacher. 5 and she said she'd never heard anything about them.

Exercise 5: 1 I went to the travel agency yesterday. 2 Are you going to buy your ticket today? 3 I'm going to buy it tomorrow. 4 I'm going to start my Italian lessons tomorrow.

Exercise 6: He asked/asked me . . . 1 if I'd/I would go to the cinema with him that evening. 2 if I was free that afternoon. 3 if I wanted to see his computer that weekend. 4 if I was busy every evening that week/last week. 5 if I was going to learn Italian this year.

Part D Exercise 2: and she said she . . . 1 had. 2 would. 3 had. 4 had. 5 would. 6 would.

Unit 13

Part A Exercise 2: 1 try . . . food 2 happen . . . someone . . . come 3 weeks . . . house . . . boat 4 desert island . . . plenty . . . time 5 how . . . start

Exercise 3: 1 Bill 2 Mike 3 Bill 4 Bill 5 Mike

Exercise 4: 2 he tried to leave the island. 3 he wouldn't build a boat. 4 and then he'd wait. 5 if he didn't do anything. 6 be happy.

Part B Exercise 4: 1 Why would Mike build a boat? 2 What would he build first? 3 Where would the boys sleep? 4 What would Bill look for?

Exercise 5: 1 would they? 2 wouldn't they?

3 wouldn't it? 4 wouldn't you? 5 would there? 6 would you?

Part C Exercise 5: *Correct order* : a d b e c

Part D Exercise 2: 1 interested 2 surprised 3 tiring 4 annoying

Unit 14

Part A Exercise 2: 1 coat 2 office 3 papers . . . desk 4 'Hello' . . . Miss Frost 5 Mr Lees . . . talking

Exercise 3: 1 to 2 to 3 not to 4 not to

Exercise 4: She's asking . . . 1 someone to show her the way. 2 Miss Frost to check an address. 3 Alan to explain something. 4 someone to help her with a machine.

Part B Exercise 2: Barbara told Sheila . . . 1 to type her letters first. 2 not to leave them until after lunch. 3 to check all the addresses. 4 not to ask Miss Frost too many questions. 5 to lock her office at night. 6 not to leave the window open.

Exercise 4: 1 Barbara told her to open the window when she arrived in the morning. 2 She told Sheila to ask her if she had a problem. 3 Alan told her to turn the computer off when she'd finished with it.

4 Miss Frost told Sheila to answer those letters at once if she could. 5 But then she told her not to worry if she couldn't start at once.

Exercise 6: 1 told 2 told 3 ordered 4 ordered

Part C Exercise 4: 1 Barbara advised her to check her spelling. 2 Barbara advised her to use a dictionary. 3 Miss Frost advised her not to believe all that Alan said. 4 Miss Frost advised her to ask Barbara if she needed help.

Exercise 5: 1 Alan told his father to sell his car. 2 Mr Lees asked Alan to suggest a price. 3 Alan advised his father not to ask for more than £150. 4 Mr Lees asked Alan to help him with an advertisement. 5 Alan advised his father to say the car was in good condition. 6 Mr Lees told Alan not to talk nonsense.

Part D Exercise 2: When I saw my new boss, I said, 'Good morning, Miss Frost.' She said, 'Hello. You're Sheila, aren't you?' Then she told me to go to her if I wanted to know anything. I didn't think she'd be so friendly.

Then she told me not to listen to Alan. She said, 'He always tells new people silly stories about me.'

Alan laughed when I told him that, and said everyone called her 'Frosty'. Now I really don't know whether he's telling the truth or not.